AF386043

CHESHIRE
COUNTY MEMORIES

DOROTHY NICOLLE was born in Uganda and later lived in Hong Kong. She was educated in Belfast and at Leicester University where she attained a degree in British Archaeology and History. She has also lived in the Middle East and in France. This gypsy life has encouraged a love of Britain and its history so that, these days, she knows that she has the perfect job - she is a Blue Badge Guide. She also lectures on various aspects of local and general history.

Chester, Queen's Park Bridge 1923 73878

CHESHIRE
COUNTY MEMORIES

DOROTHY NICOLLE

First published in hardback in 2003 as Photographic Memories of Britain - Cheshire
Revised and extended paperback edition published in the United Kingdom in 2006 by
The Francis Frith Collection as Cheshire County Memories
Paperback edition ISBN 10: 1-84589-307-7
ISBN 13: 978-1-84589-307-1

Text and Design copyright © The Francis Frith Collection®
Photographs copyright © The Francis Frith Collection®
except where indicated

The Frith® photographs and the Frith® logo are reproduced under licence from
Heritage Photographic Resources Ltd, the owners of the Frith® archive and trademarks.
'The Francis Frith Collection', 'Francis Frith' and 'Frith' are registered trademarks of
Heritage Photographic Resources Ltd.

All rights reserved. No photograph in this publication may be sold to a third party other
than in the original form of this publication, or framed for sale to a third party.
No parts of this publication may be reproduced, stored in a retrieval system, or transmitted,
in any form, or by any means, electronic, mechanical, photocopying, recording or otherwise,
without the prior permission of the publishers and copyright holder

British Library Cataloguing in Publication Data

Cheshire County Memories
Dorothy Nicolle

The Francis Frith Collection®
Frith's Barn, Teffont, Salisbury, Wiltshire SP3 5QP
Tel: +44 (0) 1722 716 376
Email: info@francisfrith.co.uk
www.francisfrith.com

Aerial photographs reproduced under licence from Simmons Aerofilms Limited
Historical Ordnance Survey maps reproduced under licence from Homecheck.co.uk

Printed and bound in England

Front Cover: **CHESTER, EASTGATE 1900** 46216t
The colour-tinting in this image is for illustrative purposes only,
and is not intended to be historically accurate

Every attempt has been made to contact copyright holders of illustrative material.
We will be happy to give full acknowledgement in future editions for any items not credited.
Any information should be directed to The Francis Frith Collection.

AS WITH ANY HISTORICAL DATABASE, THE FRANCIS FRITH ARCHIVE IS CONSTANTLY
BEING CORRECTED AND IMPROVED, AND THE PUBLISHERS WOULD WELCOME
INFORMATION ON OMISSIONS OR INACCURACIES

Contents

The Making of an Archive	8
Cheshire County Map	10
Cheshire - An Introduction	12
Chester and the West of Cheshire	16
Chester From the Air	22
The Wirral	33
Ancient Cheshire	38
Crewe and the South of Cheshire	44
Making A Living	60
Knutsford and Central Cheshire	67
Knutsford From the Air	68
Cheshire's Salt Industry	86
Warrington and the North of Cheshire	88
Cheshire Food and Recipes	106
Macclesfield and the East of Cheshire	110
Wilmslow From the Air	118
Cheshire Folklore, Sayings and Customs	124
Index	139

FRANCIS FRITH, Victorian founder of the world-famous photographic archive, was a devout Quaker and a highly successful Victorian businessman. By 1860 he was already a multi-millionaire, having established and sold a wholesale grocery business in Liverpool. He had also made a series of pioneering photographic journeys to the Nile region. The images he returned with were the talk of London. An eminent modern historian has likened their impact on the population of the time to that on our own generation of the first photographs taken on the surface of the moon.

Frith had a passion for landscape, and was as equally inspired by the countryside of Britain as he was by the desert regions of the Nile. He resolved to set out on a new career and to use his skills with a camera. He established a business in Reigate as a specialist publisher of topographical photographs.

Frith lived in an era of immense and sometimes violent change. For the poor in the early part of Victoria's reign work was a drudge and the hours long, and ordinary people had precious little free time. Most had not travelled far beyond the boundaries of their own town or village. Mass tourism was in its infancy during the 1860s, but during the next decade the railway network and the establishment of Bank Holidays and half-Saturdays gradually made it possible for the working man and his family to enjoy holidays and to see a little more of the world. With characteristic business acumen, Francis Frith foresaw that these new tourists would enjoy having souvenirs to commemorate their days out. He began selling photo-souvenirs of seaside resorts and beauty spots, which the Victorian public pasted into treasured family albums.

Frith's aim was to photograph every town and village in Britain. For the next thirty years he travelled the country by train and by pony and trap, producing fine photographs of seaside resorts and beauty spots that were keenly bought by millions of Victorians.

THE RISE OF FRITH & CO

Each photograph was taken with tourism in mind, the small team of Frith photographers concentrating on busy shopping streets, beaches, seafronts, picturesque lanes and villages. They also photographed buildings: the Victorian and Edwardian eras were times of huge building activity, and town halls, libraries, post offices, schools and technical colleges were springing up all over the country. They were invariably celebrated by a proud Victorian public, and photo souvenirs – visual records – published by F Frith & Co were sold in their hundreds of thousands. In addition, many new commercial buildings such as hotels, inns and pubs were photographed, often because their owners specifically commissioned Frith postcards or prints of them for re-sale or for publicity purposes.

In order to gain some understanding of the scale of Frith's business one only has to look at the catalogue issued by Frith & Co in 1886: it runs to some 670 pages. By 1890 Frith had created the greatest specialist photographic publishing company in the world, with over 2,000 stockists! The picture on the right shows the Frith & Co display board on the wall of the stockist at Ingleton in the Yorkshire Dales (left of window). Beautifully constructed with a mahogany frame and gilt inserts, it displayed a dozen scenes.

POSTCARD BONANZA

The ever-popular holiday postcard we know today took many years to appear, and F Frith & Co was in the vanguard of its development. Postcards became a hugely popular means of communication and sold in their millions. Frith's company took full advantage of this boom and soon became the major publisher of photographic view postcards.

Francis Frith died in 1898 at his villa in Cannes, his great project still growing. His sons Eustace and Cyril continued their father's monumental task, expanding the number of views offered to the public and recording more and more places in Britain, as the coasts and countryside were opened up to mass travel. The archive Frith created continued in business for another seventy years. By 1970 it contained over a third of a million pictures of 7,000 cities, towns and villages. The massive photographic record Frith has left to us stands as a living monument to a special and very remarkable man.

The archive's future is both bright and exciting. Francis Frith, with his unshakeable belief in making photographs available to the greatest number of people, would undoubtedly approve of what is being done today with his lifetime's work. His photographs depicting our shared past are now bringing pleasure and enlightenment to millions around the world a century and more after his death.

IRISH SEA
LANCA...
Red Ns
Liscard
Wallazey
Seacombe
Poulton
Moreton
Bidston
Gr.t Meolse
Hoose
Saughall Massey
Birkenhead with Grange
LIVERPOOL
Little Meolse
Newton with Larton
Noctorum
Claughton with Grange
WARRINGTON
To Newton
Grange
Upton
Oxton
Greasby
Tranmere
Moore
Walton Infer.
Acton Grange
Walton Super.
Grange
W.t Kirby
Frankby
Woodchurch
Prenton
Mersey
Hatton
App...
Arrow
Landican
Up.r & Low.r Bebbington
Keckwick
Daresbury
Newton by Daresbury
Caldey Grafton
Irby
Thingwell
Norton
Stockham
Thurstaston
Storeton
Spittle
Halton
Weston
Clifton or Rocksavage
Preston on the Hill
Sutton
Whitley
Pensby
Barnston
Bromborow
Aston by Sutton
Dutton
Oldfield
Brimstage
Poulton
Aston Grange
Heswall
Thornton Mayew
Eastham
Aston
River Weaver
Gayton
Raby
Hooton
FRODSHAM
Netherton
Crowton
Acton
Barting...
Leighton
Thornton Childer
Poole
Stanlow Ho.
Pier
Weston
Milton
PARKGATE
Willaston
Gr.t Stanney
Ince
Elton
Helsby
Newton
Croxton
Kingsley
Onston
Weaver...
Gr.t Neston
Lit. Neston
Little Sutton
Whitby
Hapsford
Thornton in the Moors
Dunham
Nowley
Cuddington
Ness
Great Sutton
Alvanley
Delamere
Burton
Lidsham
Lit. Stanney
Stoke
Wimbolds Trafford
Manley
Horton
DELAMERE FOREST
Puddington
Cappenhurst
Choriton
Croughton
Wervin
Pickton
Gr. Trafford
Dunham
Little Barrow
Peel Ho.
Ashton
Whitegate or New Church
Shotwick
Backford
Lea
Coughall
Tremonstall
Horton
Martou
Woodbank
Shotwick Park
Gr.t Mollington
Mickle Trafford
Great Barrow
Kelsall
Waller...
Crab Hall
Lit. Saughall
Upton
Hoole
Wallerton
Gr.t Saughall
Mollington
Newton by Chester
Guilden Sutton
Tarvin
Rockenhall
Willington
Rushton
Oulton Lo...
Blacon Ho.
CHESTER
Christleton
Dudden
Utkinton
Eaton
Dar...
New Channel
Cotton Edmunds
Bruen Stapleford
Clotton Hobfield
Little Budworth
From Holyhead
St. Marys
Rowton
Littleton
Burton
TARPORLEY
Marlston cum Leach
Claverton
Huntington
Waverton
Foulk Stapleford
Hoofield
Huxley
Tiverton
Tilston Fernall
Alpraham
Kinnerton
Eccleston
Saighton
Hatton
Chester Canal
Tarvin
Belgrave
Buerton
Golborn David
Newton
Calveley
Dodtleston
Eaton Ho.
Bruera
Golborn Bellow
Beeston
Bunbury
Aldford
Newbold
Tattenhall
Castle
Sparstow
Wardle
Palford
Lea Newbold
Handley
Peckforton
Stoke
Poulton
Aldersey
Burwardsley
Haughton
Hurleston
From Wrexham
Churton
Chowley
Harthill
Bulkeley
Ridley
Henh...
Coddington
Barton
Brindley
Farndon
Bickerton
Faddiley
Edd...
Kings Marsh
Stretton
Carden
Larkton
Preston
Cholmondeley
Bunb...
Crewe
Caldecott
Tilston
Duckington
Chorley
Baddiley
Shocklach Church
Grafton
Edgr
Frampton
Bickley
Wrenbury with Frith
Wood...
Horton
Overton
Norbury
Sou...
Shocklach Oviatt
Choriton
MALPAS
Macefen
Quasley
DENBIGHSHIRE
Cuddington
Newton juxta Malpas
Bradley
Tushingham
Marbury
River Dee
Old Castle
Wigland
Chidlow
Grindley
Newhall
Stockton
Agden
Warswall
PART OF FLINTSHIRE
From Whitchurch
From Shrewsbury
S... D...

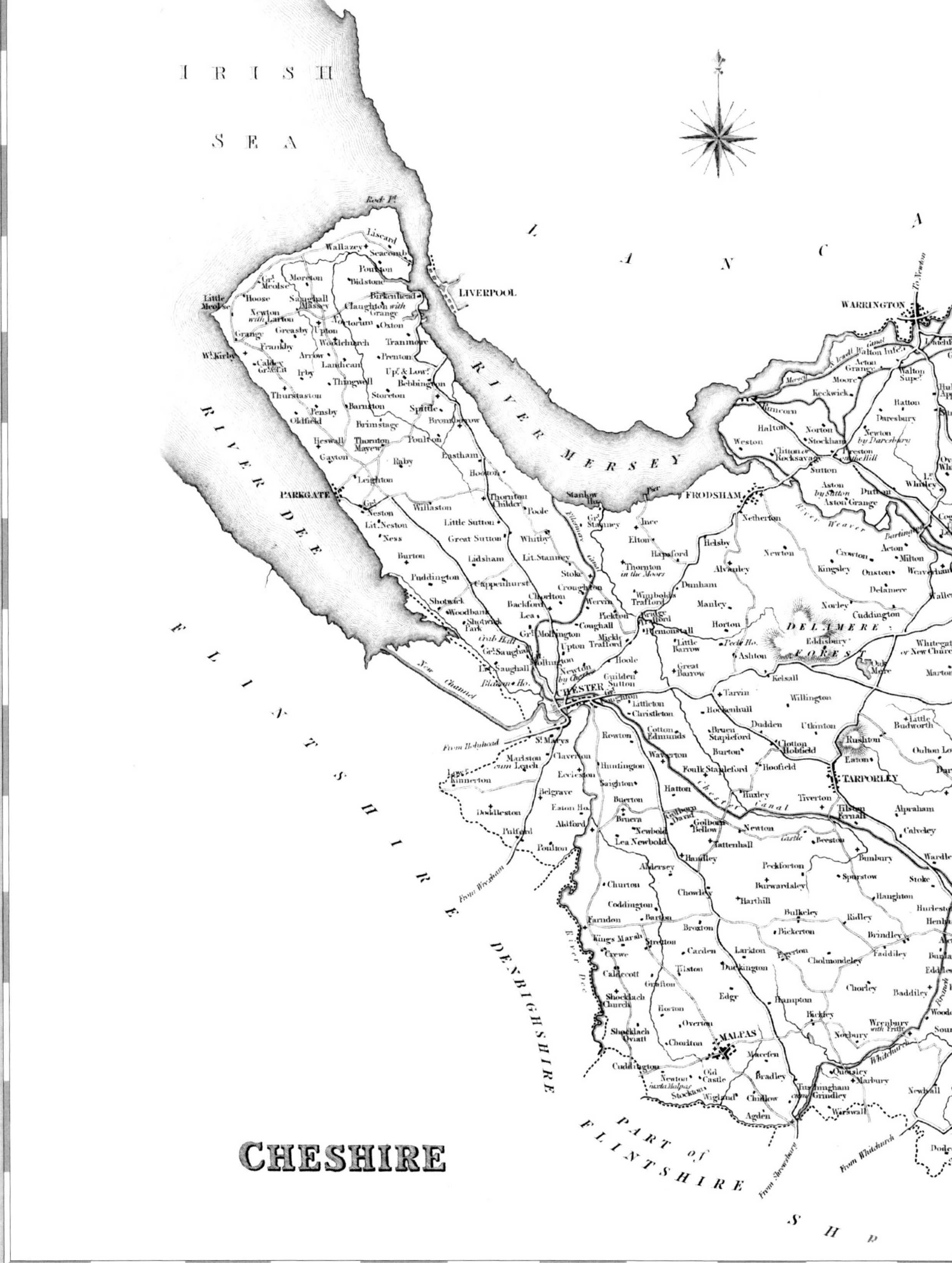

CHESHIRE

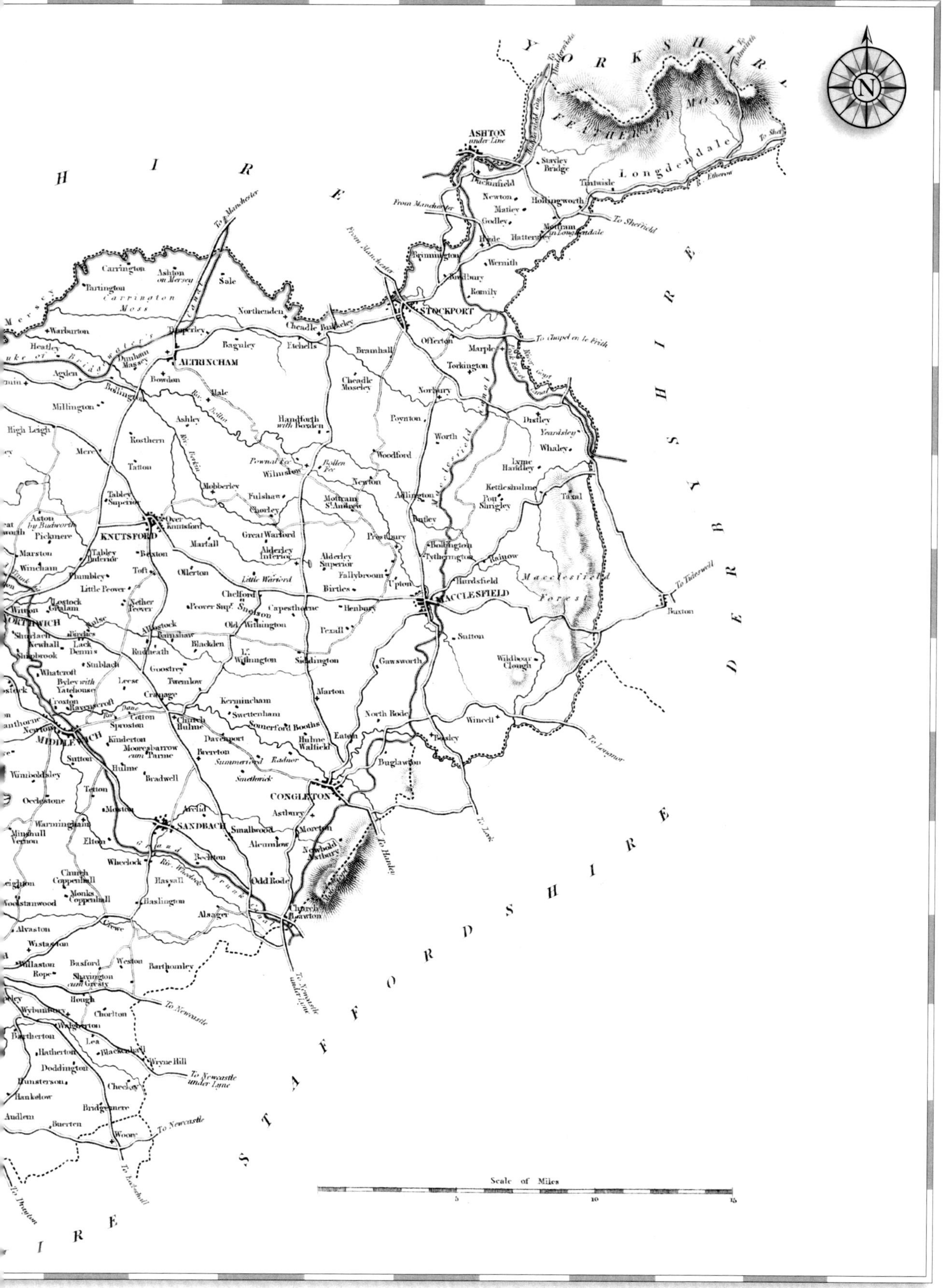

YORKSHIRE
FEATHERBED MOSS
Longdendale
N
ASHTON under Line
Staley Bridge
Tintwisle
To Etherow
To Sheffield
Dukinfield
Newton
Matley
Godley
Hollingworth
Mottram in Longdendale
Hyde
Hattersley in Longdendale
From Manchester
Brinnington
Wernith
From Manchester
Bredbury
Romily
STOCKPORT
Offerton
Marple
To Chapel en le Frith
Carrington
Ashton on Mersey
Sale
Partington
Carrington Moss
Northenden
Cheadle Bulkeley
Torkington
Timperley
Warburton
Heatley
Baguley
Etchells
Bramhall
Norbury
Disley
Agden
ALTRINCHAM
Cheadle Moseley
Yeardsley
Whaley
Dunham Massey
Bowdon
Hale
Poynton
Worth
Lyme Handley
High Leigh
Millington
Bollington
Ashley
Handforth with Boxden
Woodford
Kettleshulme
Pott Shrigley
Taxal
Mere
Rosthern
Pownal Fee
Bollin Fee
Mobberley
Wilmslow
Newton
Adlington
Butley
Tatton
Tabley Superior
Fulshaw
Chorley
Mottram St Andrew
Prestbury
Bollington
Rainow
KNUTSFORD
Over Knutsford
Great Warford
Alderley Inferior
Alderley Superior
Tytherington
To Tideswell
Aston by Budworth
Pickmere
Marthall
Fallybroom
Birtles
Upton
Hurdsfield
Macclesfield Forest
Marston
Wincham
Bexton
Toft
Little Warford
MACCLESFIELD
Witton
Plumbley
Little Peover
Nether Peover
Ollerton
Peover Sup.r
Snelson
Capesthorne
Henbury
Old Withington
Pexall
Buxton
LOSTOCK Gralam
Birches
Allostock
Rainshaw
Blackden
Sutton
NORTHWICH
Shurlach
Newhall
Lack Dennis
Rudheath
Lr. Withington
Siddington
Gawsworth
Wildboar Clough
Shipbrook
Stublach
Goostrey
Marton
Whatcroft
Byley with Yatehouse
Leese
Twemlow
Kermincham
North Rode
Wincell
To Longnor
Croxton
Ravenscroft
Cotton
Swettenham
Somerford Booths
Eaton
Anthorne
Newton
MIDDLEWICH
Sproston
Church Hulme
Davenport
Hulme Walfield
Beasley
Kinderton
Moorebarrow cum Parme
Byerton
Wimboldsley
Sutton
Hulme
Summerford Radnor
Buglawton
Occleston
Tetton
Bradwell
Smethwick
Warmingham
Moston
CONGLETON
Minshull Vernon
Elton
SANDBACH
Astbury
Smallwood
Moreton
Newbold Astbury
To Leek
Wheelock
Bechton
Alcumlow
Odd Rode
Church Coppenhall
Hassall
Baslington
Church Lawton
Woolstanwood
Monks Coppenhall
Alsager
To Hanley
Alvaston
Crewe
Wistaston
Willaston
Basford
Weston
Barthomley
Rope
Shavington cum Gresty
Hough
To Newcastle
Wybunbury
Chorlton
To Newcastle under Lyne
Walgherton
Lea
Bartherton
Hatherton
Blackenhall
Doddington
Wrine Hill
To Newcastle under Lyne
Hunsterson
Checkley
Hankelow
Bridgemere
Audlem
Buerton
Woore
To Newcastle
STAFFORDSHIRE
DERBYSHIRE
CHESHIRE
Duke of Bridgewater's Canal
River Mersey
River Bollin
River Weaver
River Dane
River Wheelock
River Trent
Scale of Miles
5
10
15

INTRODUCTION

FOLLOWING a survey carried out by a national bank in 2003, it was announced that Tatton in Cheshire 'is now the wealthiest place in Britain'. Further, the survey said, the spending power of individual salaries was also very much greater here than equivalent salaries in much of the rest of the country. A number of articles in the press followed, many of them on the theme that Cheshire is now the richest county in England. Not that Cheshire folk needed surveys of this kind to tell them something that they already knew - that the quality of life in Cheshire is better than anywhere else in the country!

Sitting on the west coast of England in what is sometimes referred to as Northern England and sometimes as Central England, according to where else in the country you live, Cheshire is a county of delightful contrasts. These range from the silted marshlands of the Wirral, to the undulating agricultural country of the south of the county with its many black and white timber houses, and on eastwards to the hill country along the edges of the Peaks; from the historic home of ancient Roman legions at Chester, to the industrial heartlands along the Mersey valley, with their many rejuvenated modern and sophisticated towns. Everywhere you go, contrasts abound and delight you.

Topographically, the county could be best divided into four distinct regions. The highest ground lies to the east, where a part of Cheshire is included in the Peak District National Park. This is sheep country, where in times past it must have been hard to make a living; it is in sharp contrast with the rich farmland of the Cheshire Plain. Geographically, most of the county is taken up in the Cheshire Plain, a landscape of low hills amongst

Macclesfield, Park Green 1897   42597

which lie numerous small lakes. This is one of the most important dairy farming areas in the country, and is the home especially of Cheshire cheese.

Further to the west is the Wirral - a long peninsula of land sticking out into the Irish Sea between the estuaries of the River Dee and the River Mersey. The eastern side of the Wirral (facing Liverpool) is now highly industrialised, but the western coastline is wonderful open countryside, much of it former marshland, and home to another smaller park, the Wirral Country Park. The north of the county is dominated by the presence of the River Mersey, which flows through it. This area has for a long time been mainly industrial, and by far the largest proportion of Cheshire's people live here.

But long before industry changed the landscape so completely, there were people already living in the area, who in their small ways made the first changes. Of necessity in those times, these early tribes would have had hilltop settlements for ease of defence, and a number of these survive - for example, the ancient hill-fort site at Helsby (see pages 40 and 105).

The first major changes to all aspects of life in the region were brought about soon after the Romans invaded Britain. Around AD79 they established a fort at a site they called Deva, because it was the lowest crossing point over the River Dee - it makes one wonder just how old the name of this river could possibly be. The legionary fortress established here covered an area of around 60 acres, and its layout has served as the ground plan for the city of Chester from that day to this.

There was a second reason for the Romans' choice of Deva as the site for their settlement: it also had excellent facilities for the establishment of a harbour. In fact, as time passed by, Chester was to become, by the Middle Ages, the most important port in all of northern England. Then disaster struck: the River Dee began to silt up. To counteract these problems, it was decided that a new

port would be built further downstream at Shotwick. But then that, too, silted up, so that a further new port was established at Burton, and then others at Neston and Parkgate. But nature has a way of winning these battles; eventually, Cheshire had to concede defeat and allow a small hamlet called Liverpool to take over as the major port for the area.

But all that was a long way in the future when, in the years following the Romans' departure from Britain, new invaders and settlers probably used the port as an easy means of access to the lands beyond. Judging by the Anglo-Saxon place-names throughout the county, the Anglo-Saxons rapidly gained the upper hand over any people already living there. England, in these years, saw the establishment of several separate kingdoms; at some time in the 7th or 8th centuries this region became part of the kingdom of Mercia. The name 'Mercia' is interesting, because it derives from an old word that meant 'border', and the name of the River Mersey has the same element; it must have been at this time, then, that the Mersey became the northern border.

By the 11th century, these English kingdoms had been divided up into administrative areas called 'shires', each one based on a major town. Hence Chester's shire came to be known as Cheshire. This system of shires as administrative regions worked wonderfully for over 1,000 years. Then in the late 20th century the growth of enormous urban districts with correspondingly large populations made them very unwieldy.

Consequently, in 1974 the ancient Saxon shire of Cheshire saw changes all along its northern border. Half of the Wirral (including the towns of Birkenhead and Wallasey) was lost to the new district known as Merseyside. Another large chunk in the north-eastern part of old Cheshire (which included towns such as Stalybridge and Stockport) was lost to Greater Manchester. In return, Cheshire acquired from Lancashire the area around and

An Introduction

including the towns of Warrington and Widnes, so that after who knows how many years, the Mersey no longer defined the border.

It was the heavy industrialisation of recent centuries within these regions that brought about this change. That is not to say, however, that Cheshire had been without industry throughout the earlier years of its existence. There is one industry that has been of major importance locally since Roman times - the salt industry. This industry was based in the centre of the county in the towns of Northwich, Middlewich and Nantwich - 'wich' in Old English meant 'salt works' - and the salt would have been taken all over the country. One has to remember the importance of salt for the preservation of food in the days before canning and freezing, not to mention the many other industries associated with it.

Salt was not the only product being transported around Cheshire and beyond. From medieval times Chester had been a major centre through which wool and cloth were exported. By the 17th century, goods were passing through the county from further afield - fragile china from the Potteries, and iron products from the new industrial centres of Shropshire and the Black Country - and these new manufactories required a steady supply of coal and other raw materials to be brought to them.

Many of these goods were moved along rivers, but the rivers were often impassable owing to floods or drought. Therefore, to begin with, work was done to make them navigable. One of the earliest rivers to be cut in this way was the River Weaver, forming what is now known as the Weaver Navigation. Then, in 1759, the Duke of Bridgewater financed the building of the first proper canal - the Bridgewater Canal. When the first stretch of this canal opened in 1761, it totally revolutionised the transportation of goods and ushered in a frenzy of canal building projects all around the country; this was only to end when it was replaced by another, similar, frenzy when railways were introduced in the following century.

Not only did the building of canals and railways bring about the easy transportation of goods, it also itself brought about a greater degree of industrialisation, as factories could be built anywhere in the country using the new steam engines to run their machines and still

Rainow c1955 R307006

be easily linked in with the transport system. The long-established skills used in the production of woollen cloth were soon used for cotton, which was imported from across the Atlantic and spun and woven in factories here. Today it is possible to see just how such a factory was worked at the Quarry Bank cotton mill at Styall near Wilmslow (see page 121). This was established in 1784. Not only is the main factory open to the public, it is also possible to see the accommodation for the apprentice children, who once worked there under the most appalling conditions.

The 20th century was to see a decline in many of the older, more traditional industries, but by and large, these have since been replaced by new ones. One type of new industry that was to dominate so many developments throughout the century was the petrochemical industry: an enormous oil refinery was developed in Stanlow near Ellesmere Port, and Runcorn and Widnes, particularly, have developed into important centres for the production of many chemically based products such as soap, glues and paints.

Another major industrial centre is Warrington. It was here that the first steam engine in Lancashire (Warrington was still part of Lancashire in those days) was installed in a cotton mill. Since then, Warrington has developed so much that it has been described as 'a town of many industries', and it is now considered to be one of the most prosperous and fast-developing towns in the county. Sad to say, Warrington has had another claim to fame in recent years: it was here that a terrorist bomb in 1993 took the lives of two young boys, and brought tragedy to so many in the town. But they will tell you that they are 'a tough lot' in Warrington; they picked themselves up and carried on, so that today, the town has a vitality and forward-looking approach that is not equalled elsewhere in Cheshire.

The last one hundred years have seen many developments in Cheshire, not least the changes to its old boundaries. But there is much that is still the same, and so gives a strong sense of identity to those who live in the Cheshire that we see today. This is still a county where both a strong rural and industrial tradition sit side by side, and perhaps it is this mix that gives the landscape its beauty and makes the towns and villages so interesting.

MARBURY, THE CHURCH AND THE MERE 1898 42478

CHESTER AND THE WEST OF CHESHIRE

Chester is sometimes referred to as 'The Walled City' as its medieval walls form the most complete circuit of medieval walls around any town or city in England. Built of red sandstone, the medieval walls form a circuit of two miles around Chester. The north and east walls follow the line of those of the old Roman fortress; those on the west and south were moved so that more land could be incorporated within the city's defences.

> ### DID YOU KNOW?
> **The Chester Imp is the name given to a grotesque figure in the north clerestory of the nave of Chester Cathedral.**

CHESTER, THE CATHEDRAL, THE WEST FRONT 1888 20577

This building was originally a Benedictine abbey. The earliest surviving remains date from around 1140, but most of the present church dates from much later. Following its dissolution during the reign of Henry VIII, the former abbey was granted cathedral status. As recently as 1975 a free-standing bell tower was completed; incidentally, this was the first to be built for an English cathedral since the 15th century.

CHESTER AND THE WEST OF CHESHIRE

Bridge Street is one of the main streets of the city of Chester, and still follows the original street plan laid down by the Romans. It is remarkable to think that St Peter's Church, at the top of the street, sits right on the site once occupied by the headquarters building (or principia) for a Roman legion. When enlarged, this photograph reveals that a couple of boys in the street are bare-footed.

CHESTER, BRIDGE STREET 1888 20596

This close-up of Bridge Street gives a clear picture of the Rows for which Chester is so famous. These consist of continuous galleries above the ground-floor level giving access to other, totally separate, shops. They probably started to develop in the form that we see them today as early as the 13th century.

DID YOU KNOW?

The title of the Earl of Chester is now conferred on the male heir to the throne of the United Kingdom, and is currently held by Prince Charles.

**A corbel on
Chester Cathedral**

CHESTER, WATERGATE STREET
1888 20608

The Rows continue around the corner and into Watergate Street. Here, just behind the horse, it is possible to see one of the many staircases that give access to the upper floor. The shop with the poultry hanging outside is now an antique shop. Notice the carving detail on the top of the building.

Venice is famous for its Bridge of Sighs, but Chester has one too - a narrow bridge over the Shropshire Union Canal, built in 1713, which linked the gaol at Northgate with the small chapel of St John, where the condemned prisoners would go for their last religious service before execution. The condemned cell in the gaol was cut out of solid rock, and was so cramped, damp and uncomfortable that it was known as 'Little Ease'.

CHESTER, QUEEN'S PARK BRIDGE 1923 73878

This photograph must have been taken when the bridge was still very new, as it was opened in April of that same year. Today sunny weather still brings people flocking to this area of the city by the riverside, although the people pictured here would probably be shocked to see the state of undress that is now considered quite normal!

CHESTER FROM THE AIR 1961 AFA92481

▼ Rowton, The Rowton Hall Hotel c1955 R90013

Built in the 18th century, the Rowton Hall Country House Hotel and Health Club, as it is now called, stands at the southern edge of the city of Chester. Despite the removal of all the ivy, and the addition of an extension on the left-hand side of the building, it is still instantly recognisable. Incidentally, the name 'Rowton' derives from the fact that this area was once considered quite rowdy!

Chester's proximity to Wales led to friction between its citizens and Welshmen in medieval times. Henry IV banned Welshmen from the streets of Chester after sunset and forbade them from carrying any weapons other than a knife for their meat.

► Eccleston
The Pump and the Church
c1955 E17003

This village's name means 'the settlement by the church', possibly in this case a church that was first founded in pre-Saxon times. Here we see the present church partially hidden amongst the trees. The pump in the foreground, with its tiled roof, was built in 1874. Notice the sign on the wall, which reads 'To Ferry'.

Eccleston, The Ferry 1895 36455

And here we see the ferry, which was attached to both sides of the river by cables and winched across. The ferry would have been capable of transporting horses, carts, waggons and coaches. Following the publication of Jerome K Jerome's book 'Three Men in a Boat', the pastime of 'messing about in boats' became very popular in Victorian and Edwardian times. Consequently the area beside the ferry crossing over the River Dee at Eccleston attracted many people. Notice how everyone is very smartly dressed, and no-one is without a hat.

Eccleston, The River Dee 1903 49887A

Eccleston
The River Dee 2003
E17701

Today just the house overlooking the river remains, and it is difficult to even imagine that there was once a wharf and steps at the other side. Boating is still popular here, although these days it is usually rowers, singly and in groups, that one sees racing up and down the river. The house is called Ferry Farm.

LITTLE SUTTON, THE SQUARE c1935 L558011

The signpost pictured here reminds us that Little Sutton straddles the main road linking Chester with Birkenhead. The posters on the wall advertise 'Pinders Big Zoo Circus', a flower show at nearby Helsby, and a British Legion 'Flower and Vegetable Show and Gala.' Notice, also, the old style of telephone box at the other side of the road. The pub on the corner is the Olde Red Lion. Today Little Sutton has become a suburb of the much newer town of Ellesmere Port.

HOOTON, THE MEMORIAL AND ST PAUL'S CHURCH c1960 H363004

Although it is the church serving the parish of Hooton, St Paul's Church sits much closer to the nearby village of Little Sutton. The brickwork of the church is really ornate, making it a wonderful example of the more florid tastes of some Victorians (it was built in 1862). Pevsner must have liked it, however - he called it 'one of the most spectacular churches in Cheshire'.

ELLESMERE PORT
THE FLOUR MILLS AND THE DOCKS C1955 E135009

Ellesmere Port was developed primarily to serve the canal that linked the towns in the region with the Mersey and Severn rivers and ultimately with the industrial heartlands of Lancashire and the Midlands. Consequently the town of Ellesmere Port could be said to date from 1 July 1795, when the Ellesmere Canal was opened. The small village of Whitby, where the canal met the river, was renamed Ellesmere Port. This photograph shows the docks that linked the Ellesmere Canal (now called the Shropshire Union Canal) with the Manchester Ship Canal, with tall flour mills in the background. Today, many of the buildings of the old docks, and the mills that lined them, have disappeared. However, this is still an important industrial area, although it is the oil refinery at Stanlow, established in 1922 just to the east of the town, which has now become more important.

ELLESMERE PORT, WHITBY ROAD C1955 E135016

It is a truism that when you want to look at the history (even the relatively recent history) of a place you should always look at the upper storeys of buildings. It is only by doing so that this photograph of Whitby Road, which was taken some fifty years ago, becomes instantly recognisable.

ELLESMERE PORT, STATION ROAD C1955 E135041

But looking at the upper floors is useless when buildings disappear altogether - as those on the right of this photograph have done. However, the bank building is still recognisable, even though the financial transactions that take place there now would make many a bank manager tremble - it is now a betting shop!

◀ ELLESMERE PORT
DOCK STREET
C1955 E135022

This is a most fascinating photograph, because the entire row of buildings on the left of the road has gone - the M53 motorway now runs right through their old back yards. Just one or two buildings on the right survive to confirm the bearings of this view, including the Horse and Jockey pub.

WILLASTON, THE GREEN c1950 W371024

The copper beech, whose leaves we can just see on the left, was planted in 1935 to commemorate the Silver Jubilee of King George V. This peaceful village developed as a group of farmhouses around a village green which until recently was rectangular in shape.

NESTON
HIGH STREET 1939
N88006

Today it is difficult to believe, but for a short time Neston was an important port: as the River Dee around Chester silted up, a new quay was built on the 'ness' or headland here in the 18th century. But this port, too, soon suffered from silting, so that today Neston is once again a relatively quiet town.

NESTON, THE CROSS c1950 N88015

The Cross is the name given to this road junction in the centre of the town, and does not refer to the drinking fountain pictured here. Even if it were plumbed in, it would be difficult to get a drink from the fountain, as it is now surrounded by a constant flow of moving traffic. It was erected in 1882 as a memorial to a local man, Christopher Bushell. Despite its grand appearance, the tower shown on the right of the photograph is really just a folly over the entrance to a house. Built of beautiful polished red Ruabon brick, and with lots of fine decorative detail on it, the local story is that it was erected simply to make this the tallest house in Neston!

PARKGATE, THE PARADE c1950 P255008

Like Neston, Parkgate saw increasing trade as a port once the River Dee around Chester began to silt up. At one time it was an important packet port for passengers travelling to Ireland, but then it too succumbed to the growing silt banks. Today the shoreline is a considerable distance away. The black and white building at the end is Mostyn House School, once the George Inn.

PARKGATE, THE PARADE
c1950 P255013

Overlooking the Gayton Sands, Parkgate now attracts bird watchers rather than travellers on their way to Ireland. Much of the land around here is now owned by the RSPB. Parkgate is so called because of an area of parkland for deer (rather than birds) that was enclosed nearby as long ago as 1250. Notice the very fine ornate lamp on the Red Lion pub on the left.

BURTON, A VIEW OF MOEL FAMMAU c1960 B561039

Taken just south of Neston, this photograph shows the view across the Dee estuary towards Wales. Even today, only forty years after this picture was taken, the estuary has become much more silted up. Where the tidal waters do reach, however, the sandbanks can be quite treacherous. Nearby are the famous Ness Botanic Gardens, maintained by the University of Liverpool.

BURTON, THE VILLAGE C1960 B561032

It is virtually impossible to believe that this landlocked village with its many beautiful old cottages was also once a port. In fact, silting has been going on for so long here that much of the land to the seaward side of the village has long since been taken over for agricultural purposes. There were five alehouses along this street some 400 years ago.

SHOTWICK, THE VILLAGE C1955 S554002

Lying at the end of a little lane that is a dead end, this is yet another former port that now lies, quite literally, some miles inland - the church even has an iron ring attached to it where once, so it is said, boats could be tied up. This is the view from the entrance to the churchyard.

THE WIRRAL

Until 1974 the Wirral was situated in Cheshire, but the boundary reforms of that year meant that much of the Wirral went to the newly created Merseyside; the new county boundary ran from just north of Ellesmere Port in the east, across to Heswall in the west. Many residents resented having to leave Cheshire, but were somewhat placated in 1986 when the government abolished Merseyside; for administrative purposes, the area became known as 'Wirral' once more. The photographs of places on the Wirral which are included in the book were all taken when their subjects were firmly in Cheshire, before 1974.

BIRKENHEAD, HAMILTON SQUARE AND TOWN SQUARE 1967 B399039

On the Wirral peninsula long stretches of sandy coastline and holiday resorts lie close to the cranes, grain elevators and oil-refinery tanks of Ellesmere Port and Birkenhead. Ellesmere Port developed and prospered with the opening of the Manchester Ship Canal, whilst Birkenhead, the largest town on the Wirral, was the dream of one man, John Laird. Around 1824 he came to a small hamlet of a few hundred people, started his shipbuilding firm, and set about planning a town. Because it was all laid out at the same time, Birkenhead was very neat and orderly. It did have areas of back-to-back houses for the newly imported workers, but there were never the slums of the older towns and cities. Birkenhead's Hamilton Square, which was completed in 1826, has the largest number of Grade 1 listed buildings in England in one place, with the exception of Trafalgar Square in London. Birkenhead Park, which was completed in 1846, was the first park in the country to be provided at public expense. It was designed by Joseph Paxton, the famous head gardener of Chatsworth.

Birkenhead, The Docks 1967 B399038

Birkenhead Docks were started on 23 October 1844, when the foundation stone was laid. Before that, ships sheltered or tied up in Bidston Pool. The Docks were once an independent company, but money troubles forced them to join the Mersey Docks & Harbour Board and to be controlled from Liverpool. The arrival of the railway in the 1840s made the need for deep water docks even more essential. The Great Western Railway ran into Birkenhead and the Docks, and the London Midland Scottish Railway ran into Liverpool. Birkenhead's Great Float Dock provided employment directly and indirectly for over one hundred years before competition from Europe and improvements in road transport sent it into decline. In recent years substantial government and private funding has been invested in Birkenhead; the land at the eastern end of the Great Float has been developed as the Twelve Quays, and the port is now the terminal for cargo and passenger services between Merseyside and Ireland. A floating stage can work with two roll-on/roll-off ferries at the same time. The ferries can save an hour on an Irish Sea crossing as they no longer have to travel through Liverpool's enclosed dock system.

Birkenhead contains the oldest standing building on Merseyside - Birkenhead Priory, whose Benedictine monks were granted a charter around 1150 to run the first ferry across the River Mersey.

Birkenhead, The Queensway Tunnel c1965 B399027

The Queensway Tunnel, which was opened by George V and Queen Mary on 18 July 1934, was the first of the two road traffic tunnels to be dug under the Mersey; it soon replaced the car ferries and luggage boats. Some 200,000 people gathered to watch the event, and 80,000 of those celebrated with a 'tunnel walk' through from Liverpool to Birkenhead.

A most unusual feature can be found in the porch of Christ Church at High Bebington, on the Wirral. A dinosaur footprint, which was found in some sandstone rock from the old Storeton stone quarries, has been set into the wall of the tower porch of Christ Church.

NEW BRIGHTON, THE BEACH 1887 20067

New Brighton was developed from open waste space, and was laid out specifically to be an attraction. James Atherton was the man with the dream, helped and supported by John Askew. Although the original plans were very grand and exciting, money proved a problem. Costs kept on rising before income started to come in, the large mansions planned became ordinary houses, and the exclusive hotels became boarding houses and cafés. Also known as Perch Rock and the Battery, the Fort was, and still is, a very large landmark on the New Brighton shore. Completed in 1825 at a cost of £25,000, it was part of the defences on the River Mersey, and was used to store gunpowder for ships visiting Liverpool. It is now used as a museum.

NEW BRIGHTON, THE TOWER AND THE SANDS 1900 45163

An Eiffel-style Tower at New Brighton was always part of the original dream of James Atherton as he planned his new holiday resort. It was started in 1896 and opened in 1898. At 631ft high, it was the tallest structure in England at the time. Sadly, money was short, and maintenance was haphazard. During the First World War the tower was allowed to rot, and in 1918 it was declared unsafe. No money could be found to repair the tower, so in 1919 work started on dismantling it. By Easter 1921 it was gone. The building below the tower lasted until it was destroyed by fire in 1969.

THE WIRRAL

NEW BRIGHTON, THE LIGHTHOUSE 1892 30413

Tradition says that a lighthouse was built on the sands at New Brighton in the early 1700s, but it collapsed into the sand. A ship carrying cotton bales was shipwrecked off the Wirral, and the bales washed ashore. Wood and parts of the ship soon sank into the sand, but the bales of cotton did not. Then grass started to grow in the cotton bales, and this held firm in the sand. Bales of cotton were then deliberately sunk into the foreshore, and a wall was built on them. They did not sink, and the two lighthouses along this shore were built on the same principle: Leasowe first, then New Brighton in 1827 at a cost of £27,000. This photograph shows that the entrance was 40ft up the lighthouse, and could only be reached by climbing up an iron ladder fixed to the outside of the 90ft structure. In the late 1980s the lighthouse was sold, refurbished and subsequently marketed as a quirky site for honeymooners and those wanting something different for a weekend break.

The last light beamed out across Liverpool Bay from Moreton Lighthouse on the Wirral on 15 July 1908, when the last recorded keeper was a Mrs Williams, the only known woman lighthouse keeper of her time. After a period as a tearoom, the building remained derelict until 1989, when it was restored and converted into an information centre and Ranger office for the North Wirral Coastal Park.

EGREMONT, FROM THE SANDS 1895 36685

Egremont was never as commercial as its sister New Brighton, but it was still a popular holiday destination. The black and white timber building on the left of this photograph was Old Mother Redcap's Inn, which was steeped in history. The inn was popular with sailors and smugglers, who left their pay and prize money with Mother Redcap to keep safe in various hiding places. After Mother Redcap's death very little money or gold was found in the inn; local tradition says that there is still gold buried somewhere in this area, and that one day a large hidden cache of treasure may well be found! The inn was pulled down in the 1970s, but the ghost of Old Mother Redcap is said to haunt the area, looking for the sailors' gold that she hid away.

Right: WALLASEY, THE DOCKS
c1965 W164088

Wallasey Docks were built on what was known as Wallasey Pool, a once wild and beautiful tidal creek. The first boilermaking and shipbuilding yard was established by William Laird (the father of John Laird who developed Birkenhead) in the mid 1820s. In 1829 William Laird launched his first iron ship, a 60-ton lighter for use in Ireland. Dock development in Wallasey Pool continued at a pace from then on, with Egerton and Morpeth Docks opening in 1847, Alfred Dock being finished in 1851 and Wallasey Dock opening in 1877. From 1945, the number of people employed by the shipbuilding yards in Wallasey and Birkenhead declined and a number of associated industries closed. To offset this, other trades began to expand and diversify, and new factories opened. Wallasey Docks became the main grain importing area for Merseyside. The Homepride Flour Mills can be seen in this photograph, and the vessel on the left of the photograph is a cargo boat registered in Karachi, probably delivering grain from Asia.

Below Right: WALLASEY
ST HILARY'S CHURCH AND THE TOWER c1873
8468

The old Wirral village of Wallasey has developed slowly, and even today there are still some of the older buildings dotted around. The Wirral was colonised by Norsemen long ago, and many names reflect those invaders who settled here - Wallasey means 'the low land (or island) where the Welsh live'. St Hilary's is the old parish church of Wallasey. There are not many churches dedicated to this saint, and this particular church is unique because of its two towers. There has been a church on this site for over a thousand years. A fire has twice destroyed the buildings: the lone tower dates from a church built in or around 1530, which caught fire in the 1850s. The tower was saved, and the new church, seen behind, was built slightly away from the old tower. The older tower is noted for its gargoyles.

Though fishing was the principal industry of the village of Wallasey, James Stonehouse, who knew the area in the late 17th century, portrayed the inhabitants as a shifty lot who made their real livings through less legal means. He wrote that 'the inhabitants were nearly all wreckers and smugglers - they ostensibly carried on the trade and calling of fishermen, farm-labourers and small farmers; but they were deeply saturated with the sins of covetousness, and many a fierce fire has been lighted on the Wirral shore on stormy nights to lure the good ships on the Burbo or Hoyle Banks. There is scarcely a house in the north Wirral that could not provide a guest with a good stiff glass of brandy or Hollands.' Perhaps that explains why it was said that the flames had the blue haze of burning brandy on one of the occasions when St Hilary's Church burnt down!

ANCIENT CHESHIRE

DID YOU KNOW?

In the Earth's History Gallery of Warrington Museum and Art Gallery are some rare footprints of a dinosaur known as chirotherium, which existed in the Warrington area a staggering 240 million years ago.

THE BRIDESTONES, shown in photograph T219010, are the remains of a Neolithic chambered tomb, believed to date back to around 3,000BC, and are often described as Cheshire's only megalithic monument. The tomb was aligned east to west, and originally had a covering mound and two other chambers. All that is left today is the main chamber, but the tomb is believed to have had a horned cairn and crescentic forecourt. It was excavated in the 18th century.

There are several theories as to how the tomb acquired its name, one being that it relates to the ancient fertility goddess Bride. An old legend says that the stones are the petrified members of a wedding party, whilst Jacqueline Simpson's 'Folklore of the Welsh Border' (1976) notes a story from Ingram's 'Companion into Cheshire' (1947) that a Viking was buried here with his bride, a local Saxon girl. Yet another explanation is that the name is the result of a wedding that was held here in the 1930s!

One of the earliest industrial sites in Cheshire was at Tatton Park at Knutsford, where archaeological excavations have found evidence of a Middle Stone Age flint-working site.

TIMBERSBROOK, THE BRIDESTONES C1955 T219010

ALDERLEY EDGE, ENGINE VEIN 2005 A29701

Alderley Edge in Cheshire is one of the most important archaeological sites in the country. Local people had always believed that ancient mining activity had taken place at the Edge but this was not confirmed until a wooden shovel was rescued by the local author Alan Garner from the rubbish under the stage at Alderley Edge Primary School in the early 1950s. The shovel was dated in 1993 to the early Bronze Age, 1,850-1,750BC, providing modern archaeologists with scientific evidence. After this discovery the Manchester Museum and National Trust conducted an excavation beside Engine Vein in 1997 (see photograph A29701), and carbon dating there confirmed that Alderley Edge is the site of the earliest known copper mine in England. The wooden shovel is now in Manchester Museum, although it is not yet on permanent display. Bronze Age material has also been found in Wilmslow. When the railway was built in 1841-42, workmen found the remains of burial urns holding cremated bones when they dug the foundations for the viaduct over the Bollin, and when the second runway was built at Manchester Airport, a Bronze Age settlement was revealed and excavated. All these signs suggest a flourishing community in the area.

Moving on 1,800 years or so, and the Iron Age has left even grimmer reminders of itself in the remains of Lindow Man, who was sacrificed by the Celtic people of the Wilmslow area in the 1st century AD. His body, apparently ritually murdered and offered to the gods, was left in the watery peat bog of Lindow Moss, a landscape on the borders of earth and water. He had been in the prime of life, and was possibly sacrificed to try and ward off the Romans, who were invading Cheshire at this time - if so, then it was a futile and tragic effort to postpone the inevitable.

WILMSLOW, LINDOW MOSS c1955 W103010

In 1995 a suspicious-looking depression appeared beside Engine Vein on Alderley Edge, and the Derbyshire Caving Club, which has an arrangement with the National Trust to maintain the mines under the Edge, moved in to cap what was recognised as a collapsing mine shaft. Four feet down the shaft they found a 4th-century Roman coin hoard, still in the broken pot in which it had been buried. It was not a high value hoard; analysis of the coins showed it probably represented a poor man's life savings, buried for safety at a time of unrest, but never retrieved. One wonders what happened to the person who buried the pot but never came back for it.

Archaeologists and the Derbyshire Caving Club excavated the shaft, now named Pot Shaft, and retrieved a quantity of lead mining spoil, as well as a number of Bronze Age hammer stones. Forty feet down, they came to the bottom of the shaft and discovered that it linked with a short passage into Engine Vein itself. At the very bottom of Pot Shaft was a drainage sump, and in it, saturated with water, they found some oak planks. The wood was carbon dated and found to date from the mid 1st century AD, the earliest period of Roman occupation of Britain. Here was proof that as soon as the Romans conquered the Cheshire area, they were up on Alderley Edge mining lead. Perhaps they hoped to find silver, as they had on the Mendips in Somerset, but even though there were no precious metals the lead was extremely useful to the Romans, given their liking for good plumbing. It probably also provided the metal for the evaporating pans at the strategically important salt works a few miles away in what are now Northwich and Middlewich. Northwich ('Condate') and Middlewich ('Salinae') were both garrisoned by the Romans during the late 1st century. The forts at both towns were situated close to major road junctions but it is also probable that these installations served in the additional role of guarding the salt workings, collecting dues and regulating trade.

ANCIENT CHESHIRE

> ### DID YOU KNOW?
>
> *The name for the Roman fort at Northwich was 'Condate'. It was built on Castle Hill, close to the point where the Rivers Dane and Weaver join, and where the military road between Chester and Manchester crossed the Weaver. The name 'Condate', meaning 'confluence', may indicate the worship locally of the Celtic god Condatis, the guardian of water meeting, as it was customary to pray to the water spirits before crossing.*

FRODSHAM
HELSBY ROCK FROM OVERTON C1965 F176034

Helsby Rock is an Iron Age promontory hillfort of the Celtic people of pre-Roman Britain, which appears to have been in use from around 800BC to AD43. It was protected by natural steep slopes on the west and north sides, and by man-made earth and stone ramparts on the more gently sloping south side.

The modern city of Chester stands on historic foundations. The strategic importance of the site now occupied by the city was realised by the Romans during their campaigns against the Brigantes and the tribes of north Wales. They established a fort which they called Deva on the north bank of the River Dee, at the lowest bridging point before the estuary. Their fort covered an area of around 60 acres, and comprised an outer ditch and a turfed rampart topped by a wooden palisade, together with wooden gatehouses and towers. Capable of holding a legion (5-6,000 men), the huge fortress was completed in AD79-80, but reconstruction work was begun at some time around AD100 to make the fort a more permanent settlement. Much of modern Chester follows the ground plan of the Roman settlement that was first established here in the 1st century.

CHESTER, BRIDGE STREET 1903 49889

Deva (Chester) was the headquarters of the Twentieth Legion, 'Legio XX Valeria Victrix' - the name properly means 'Conquering Eagle,' but is usually given as 'Valiant and Victorious'. The Roman fortress of Deva contained the usual buildings associated with an important military establishment: headquarters, barracks, bath-house, latrines, hospital, gymnasium, granaries, workshops, storage and equipment sheds. A civilian settlement grew up outside the walls, and stretched along what is now Foregate Street. Also outside the walls, to the south-east, was the amphitheatre, which was built around AD86 and could seat 8,000 spectators, making it the largest stone amphitheatre uncovered in Britain. Although part of the amphitheatre now lies underneath the grounds of a neighbouring convent, it is still possible to walk into the arena through one of the surviving entrances, and imagine the wild beast fights and gladiatorial combats that took place there in Roman times. One of the features of this amphitheatre was a shrine to Nemesis, the Roman goddess of vengeance, to whom gladiators would pray and make offerings before their fights, sometimes to the death. The original altar is now in the Grosvenor Museum in Chester, but a replica has been erected in the arena.

> ### DID YOU KNOW?
> *Repairs to Chester's city walls in the 1800s uncovered over 100 Roman tombstones, which had been built into the walls. Examples of these memorials can be seen in the Grosvenor Museum.*

CHESTER, THE WATER TOWER AND THE ROMAN HYPOCAUST 1888 20616

The Water Tower in Chester was built in 1322 as an outwork to the tower on the north-west corner of the city wall. The tower derives its name from the time when Chester was a thriving port and ships used to moor alongside it. This photograph shows the remains of a Roman hypocaust, the heating system for a Roman bath, which were discovered in Bridge Street in 1863 and subsequently relocated to the gardens by the Water Tower.

> ### DID YOU KNOW?
> *In Warrington Museum and Art Gallery is a Roman actor's mask, which was found at Wilderspool. It is the only example found in Britain.*

Warrington's diverse industrial tradition began in the Roman period; a Roman settlement was established in the Wilderspool area around AD100, which was known as Veratinum. For most of the period of Roman Britain this settlement became an important industrial centre, and metal products, glass and pottery were made here and in Northwich and Middlewich, which together with Wilderspool served as supply bases for the Roman military to the north. A pottery kiln in the area was operated by a person who stamped the name 'Maco' on his wares. In fact, so industrious was this part of Cheshire that it has been referred to as the Roman Black Country.

SANDBACH, ANCIENT SAXON CROSSES
C1955 S489016

In the Market Square of Sandbach are the shafts of two stunningly beautiful carved Saxon crosses. The taller shaft is covered with scenes from the life of Christ, whilst the smaller is thought to depict scenes from the life of King Penda of Mercia, whose territory this once was. He was converted to Christianity some time around AD653. First recorded in 1565 as 'two square crosses on stone steps with certain images and writing thereon graven', these superb crosses were destroyed by Puritans in the following century. Since then, the broken pieces that survived have been gathered together and restored as far as is possible. A number of other Saxon cross shaft fragments can also be found in St Mary's churchyard in Sandbach.

The Church of St Mary and St Helen in Neston houses parts of five decorated late Saxon crosses. The carvings depict a figure of a priest, figures of two horsemen and two other figures fighting with daggers.

Photograph 40446 (below) shows three Saxon pillar crosses which can be found in Macclesfield's West Park. The crosses date from the late 9th or early 10th centuries, and feature some weathered interlace decoration. The crosses are not on their original sites - two came from Ridge Farm, Wincle, and the other came from Upton. They are of a type that is found on the Cheshire Plain and the Peak District, and their original purpose may have been as boundary markers of the territory of the Anglo-Saxon kingdom of Mercia.

MACCLESFIELD, WEST PARK 1897 40446

DID YOU KNOW?

In Anglo-Saxon times a church dedicated to St Werburgh stood on part of the site now occupied by Chester's cathedral. St Werburgh was a daughter of King Wulfhere of Mercia. Werburgh was supervisor of all the nunneries of Mercia, and died at Trentham in AD699. In AD874 St Werburgh's remains were transferred to Chester to prevent them falling into the hands of Danish invaders.

PRESTBURY, THE NORMAN CHAPEL 1896 37443

The doorway of the chapel at Prestbury is one of the oldest Norman ecclesiastical examples in Cheshire, and is famous for the zigzag patterns and beaked heads carved on the arch. Restoration work was carried out on the chapel in the 18th century, when a new roof was added.

LOWER PEOVER, THE CHURCH C1955 L308011

Despite the stone tower that the visitor sees first, it is the timberwork of St Oswald's Church at Lower Peover that makes it so noteworthy. The early timberwork has not been accurately dated, but the church was founded in 1269. If this timberwork dates from that first church, as is thought possible, this could well be one of the oldest arcaded wooden frame churches in Europe.

BEESTON, THE CASTLE C1955 B57054

BEESTON, THE CASTLE ENTRANCE C1955 B57059

Beeston Castle's name tells us that originally this marvellous hilltop site was somewhere where commerce took place. It has been a fortified site since Celtic times, although the castle whose ruins we see today dates from the 1200s, when it was one of a series of castles all along the English-Welsh border. Although it had fallen into disrepair by the time of the Civil War, the castle was then refortified; it changed hands several times during the war, and was finally slighted to make it of no further military use in 1645. It was taken over by the Ministry of Works (the ancestor of today's English Heritage) in 1959, and now has a very good little museum within the garden area. The castle is perhaps best known for the treasure that was supposedly hidden here by Richard II in 1399 on his way to Ireland. On his return he was captured by the forces of the future Henry IV, and met his death in Pontefract Castle soon afterwards. Searches have been made, but nothing has ever been found!

RKS & SPENCER
LITTLEWOODS
LIPTON
DUDD & Cº

CREWE AND THE SOUTH OF CHESHIRE

CREWE, MARKET STREET AND THE SQUARE
c1955 C316030

In the 17th century, Daniel King described the county and people of Cheshire in the following words: 'The air is very wholesome (so) that the people of the country are seldom infected with diseases or sickness ... The people there live till they be very old; some are grandfathers, their fathers yet living; and some be grandfathers before they be married ... The people of the country are of nature very gentle and courteous ... they are stout and hardy; of stature tall and mighty ... the women are very friendly and loving ... and in all kinds of house-wifery expert, fruitful in bearing of children, after they be married, and sometimes before'. (From 'The Vale Royal of England', published in 1656.)

Less than two hundred years ago this was farmland. Then the railways arrived. By the end of the 1800s there were 40,000 people living here, all linked in some way with the important railway junction that had developed. The fact that Crewe was a new town with a relatively young population is, sad to say, reflected in the number of names that surround the war memorial in the foreground.

CREWE AND THE SOUTH OF CHESHIRE

CREWE, MARKET STREET C1955 C316027

Despite the fact that this part of Crewe has seen enormous development and regeneration in recent years, this view is still instantly recognisable. Burton's continues to occupy the building on the right. The building on the left in this picture, however, has been completely replaced.

CREWE, THE CHETWODE ARMS AND ST PAUL'S CHURCH C1950 C316013

On the other hand, the view here has completely changed. The road beside St Paul's Church has been widened, and in the process the pub has gone, and so have all the terraced houses that can be seen beyond. The church still survives (without that lovely slender spire), but the building is no longer used for religious purposes.

CREWE, THE MAIN ENTRANCE, QUEEN'S PARK C1950 C316002

Renowned as one of the finest parks in the north of England, Queen's Park was given to the town by the London and North Western Railway Company to commemorate fifty years of the railway in the town. Originally on the edge of town, nowadays it is completely surrounded by new housing estates. This view of the main gates is taken from inside the park.

CREWE, THE ROLLS-ROYCE WORKS c1965 C316093

Although it was undoubtedly the railways that first brought heavy industry to the Crewe region (indeed they were for a long time the major employers in the town), it was not long before other industries associated with engines and heavy machinery followed. The most famous of these was Rolls-Royce, shown here, whose Aero Engine factory was established in 1938. Throughout the Second World War the company produced engines for Spitfires, Hurricanes, Lancasters and Mosquitoes. After the Second World War, it was for the production of cars that this factory became famous; for a time road signs in the vicinity all advertised 'Crewe and Nantwich - Home of the Best Cars in the World'.

HASLINGTON, HIGH STREET c1955 H324004

There are claims, however unlikely, that nearby Haslington Hall was built using timbers that had been salvaged from Spanish galleons captured at the time of the Armada. The building in the centre of the picture, however, claims to be even older - it has the date of 1510 proudly displayed above the front door.

◄ NANTWICH
THE SQUARE C1965 N3041

Traditionally Nantwich was the most important of Cheshire's three salt towns, although salt production ceased here in the 1800s. The salt brought great wealth to the town, exemplified by its many lovely black and white timbered buildings. This photograph shows the western end of the Square. There are few genuinely old buildings in Nantwich, because most were destroyed in a severe fire during the reign of Elizabeth I. However, there are some fine Georgian and Victorian buildings - one is the bank at the far side, peeping out behind the trees. It was built in 1866, and was then the Liverpool and Manchester District Bank.

NANTWICH, THE PARISH CHURCH 1898 42187

This stunningly beautiful church is known as 'the cathedral of south Cheshire'. In fact it is the only church in Cheshire that Simon Jenkins in his recent book 'England's Thousand Best Churches' placed in his top 100. Yet until the 16th century it was just a chapel of ease for nearby Acton church, which was considered to be far more important. Having survived the great fire of Nantwich of 1583, the church, dedicated to St Mary, is the oldest building in the town. Much of the structure dates from the 14th century, although it is thought that building work was probably interrupted by the Black Death, and only resumed much later that same century. The church was restored (some say excessively) in 1855-79 by Sir George Gilbert Scott, and below the fine octagonal crossing tower there is today a particularly fine crossing vault to his design.

The carved misericords in Nantwich's parish church are quite delightful, with depictions of exotic animals, a mermaid, and even a comic carving of a woman beating her husband with a ladle.

NANTWICH, WELSH ROW c1965 N3070

Separated from the main part of the town by the River Weaver, Welsh Row is, as its name tells us, the road leading towards Wales. Welsh cattle drovers would have come this way in order to trade their animals in the market for salt.

NANTWICH, HIGH STREET 1898 42179

This part of the town was devastated by the fire of 1583, so that everything here was rebuilt after that date. For instance, the timber building on the right with the 'spike' on the gable end was built the following year. It has an inscription that reads:

> *God grant our ryal Queen*
> *In England long to raign*
> *For she hath put her helping*
> *Hand to bild this town again.*

Elizabeth I donated money of her own to help rebuild Nantwich, and also encouraged a nationwide find-raising appeal for its rebuilding, showing how important the town, and its salt industry, was to the country's economy.

ACTON, ST MARY'S CHURCH
1898 42197

St Mary's Church is one of the finest churches in Cheshire, and serves a community that was, at one time, more important than nearby Nantwich. The phrase 'the weakest go to the wall' reminds us of a time when churches did not provide their congregation with seats or pews. Some churches, however, had seats built into the wall for the elderly and infirm, and here they still survive.

WRENBURY, THE GREEN c1955 W414004

The 'fortified settlement where wrens could be found' is still a peaceful place, with wrens undoubtedly still around. But this spot has not always been peaceful - the village green not only served as common ground for local people to graze their animals, but was also the venue for bear baiting in the past. The black and white building pictured here was replaced, in 1960, by a modern brick house.

Overlooking the village green at Wrenbury is St Margaret's Church. One notable curiosity inside is the old dog whipper's pew. Paid a few shillings a year (and given a coat and hat), the dog whipper's job was to keep all the dogs that were brought into church during services by their owners under control, and also to ensure that the congregation stayed awake.

WRENBURY
THE DOCTOR'S HOUSE
C1955 W414005

Now called Stanley House, this beautiful timber-framed house is relatively recent compared to many in the area - above the window in the gable end there is a plaque that reads '1859.' In fact, a close look at the house reveals that it is not a timber-framed building at all - the black detail has all been painted onto the walls.

The extremely pretty village of Marbury is in the heart of what was once Cheshire's cheese-producing country. Milk is still produced here, but the cheese is now made in local factories rather than on the farms.

MARBURY, THE CHURCH
1898 42480

St Michael's Church stands on a prominent site overlooking the mere; Marbury means 'a fortified place by a lake'. In fact it sits between two small lakes, making it a well defended site from possible Welsh attack - the border is only three or four miles away. Not that this would be so effective today, as the lake has almost completely dried up. If you look closely at the church, you might think you see a slight lean of the tower - and you could be right. Built on sandstone, with the mere just beneath it, the church has slipped slightly over the years; today the 63ft tower apparently tilts more than two feet out of the vertical. There is a local legend that says that if the ancient yew tree in the churchyard falls, so will the church.

◀ MALPAS, THE CROSS
c1955 M281021

This small town is unusual in that its name derives totally from French. 'Mal pas' means 'bad step or way' or 'difficult passage'. Perhaps early Normans were set upon as they travelled here, or perhaps they just found the terrain difficult. Whatever its failings as a route in the past, it was later to become an important stop for stagecoaches travelling between Chester and London.

CHESHIRE

◄ MALPAS
THE CROSS 1898
42485

Notice how the children stand unconcernedly in the middle of the road in this charming photograph! The cross in the foreground was erected in 1877; it commemorates Charles Augustus Thurlow, who was rector here for 33 years. The black and white building at the far side of the street is the Victoria Jubilee Hall, erected in 1887; today it also has a clock to celebrate another jubilee, that of Elizabeth II in 2002.

▲ CHOLMONDELEY, THE CASTLE AND THE PARK 1898 42483

Nothing is quite what it seems here. Despite its spelling, the name is pronounced 'Chumley'. Despite its looks, the castle actually only dates from 1801, when the main house was built; the turrets and towers were then added even later in 1817. The architect who did this later work, Robert Smirke, is also known for another 'fake' castle he designed at Eastnor in Herefordshire.

◄ CHOLMONDELEY
NANTWICH LODGE
c1940 C98001

This delightful little gatehouse has not changed at all. It sits by an entrance on the south of the estate. The estate covers around 800 acres, and includes gardens which have been described as 'the most romantically beautiful' - they were largely laid out in the 19th century, although they were extensively replanted in the 1960s.

BUNBURY, THE VILLAGE C1960 B562016

Bunbury is a name familiar to those of us who enjoy Oscar Wilde's 'The Importance of Being Earnest', but few people realise that such a village actually exists. Fortunately for Bunbury's continued tranquillity, the main road totally bypasses it, so that it can be very pleasant to sit on the bench here on a sunny day. The hedge behind has now grown so that it is the same height as the signpost, making the garden much more secluded! This area is, or rather was, the village green. The house in the centre was built in 1831, and incorporates what was once the village lock-up, with the old cells now forming part of the entrance hall.

BUNBURY, TUDOR COTTAGE
C1960 B562009

Bunbury has been described as 'a village that the commuter has found but not spoilt', and it has a delightful mixture of buildings of all periods. The village itself is rather a tale of two halves: the area around the village green has the shops, and the other half, a short distance away, is focused on the church.

CREWE AND THE SOUTH OF CHESHIRE

BUNBURY, THE DYSART ARMS
C1960 B562007

Here we see the pub where all village pubs should be - next door to the churchyard. St Boniface's is an imposing church, and dates from the 14th century, although the builders appear to have used stones from an earlier church on the site. It is also the home of the oldest alabaster tomb in Cheshire - that of Sir Hugh Calveley - which dates to 1394.

During the Second World War the town of Crewe was a prime target for air attacks, and the villages nearby did not escape. In 1940 bombs fell in this part of Bunbury, and the church was nearly destroyed. Barrage balloons were used to try and protect Crewe, but these were not always successful - on one occasion a direct hit on the Rolls-Royce factory killed 16 workers.

TARPORLEY, THE OLD MANOR HOUSE C1955 T218012

Tarporley has an extremely attractive main street. At its southern end sits the Manor House. There are two inscriptions on this building: one is just below the crest on the left gable, and the second is underneath the window just below it. The top inscription gives a date for the building of 1586, and the one below says 1585!

LITTLE BUDWORTH, ST PETER'S CHURCH
c1960 L310001

Little Budworth is normally a very peaceful little village. Within its parish lies one of the few remaining survivals of genuinely ancient forest and heathland, now a Site of Special Scientific Interest. It can, however, be very noisy here at times - the parish is now also home to the Oulton Park motor racing circuit.

CHURCH MINSHULL, ST BARTHOLOMEW'S CHURCH c1955 C478003

A close inspection of the brickwork of St Bartholomew's Church reveals the date when the tower was built - 1702. The main body of the church was completed two years later. The previous church had been timber-framed and the village still has a number of timber-framed buildings; there is a particularly pretty one just across the street from the church.

CHURCH MINSHULL
THE OLD MILL C1955 C478006

Now used as a forge, the old mill at Church Minshull was originally used for the grinding of corn. The old water wheel in the mill was also once used to provide electricity for the whole village, which only joined the National Grid around 1960. Miss Billenge, who then ran the mill, always kept the wheels turning to provide the power, although at times lights would flicker throughout the village if too much power was being used at any one time.

SANDBACH, THE BLACK BEAR INN AND THE MARKET PLACE C1955 S489009

Sandbach's Square is the scene, each May, of an Elizabethan market held to commemorate the original market charter presented to the town in the 1500s. The Saxon crosses are just behind the Black Bear pub on the left, which has the date of 1634 just above the entrance. The structure on the right is the war memorial.

CREWE AND THE SOUTH OF CHESHIRE

▼ SANDBACH, OLD HOUSES C1955 S489017

This view has altered considerably. The brick building on the right has gone, and the timber building beside it has been extended. The building on the left, however, has hardly changed - it is the Lower Chequer pub, thought to be the oldest building in the town, built in 1570. Notice the platform just beside the entrance from where riders could mount their horses.

▶ ALSAGER, CREWE ROAD C1965 A214021

At first this view looks typical of many streets in small towns all over the country; and yet just behind the buildings on the left is Alsager Mere, which is most attractive. Until recently Alsager was primarily an agricultural village, which is most appropriate - its name means 'the cultivated land of a man called Aelle'.

CREWE AND THE SOUTH OF CHESHIRE

Picturesque this certainly is. Unfortunately, it is also a fake. The ruin was built in the 1700s by Randle Wilbraham to enhance his view from Rode Hall at Scholar Green, where he lived. It later became a meeting place for early Methodists. Today the site is protected by the National Trust.

▶ LITTLE MORETON HALL FROM THE EAST 1897 40474

Known all over the world from pictures on calendars, cards and tourist brochures, Little Moreton Hall is the finest moated half-timbered house in the country. Its survival in its near-original form probably owes much to the fact that its owners were often very stretched for cash and could never therefore afford to alter it, add bits on to it or change it in any way, fortunately for us today.

MAKING A LIVING

INDUSTRY came early to Cheshire. It is known that copper ore was being extracted from Alderley Edge as early as 2,000BC. The Edge itself is a wooded sandstone cliff stretching some two miles in length and rising to around 650ft. There are a number of surface workings, such as those at Stormy Point, which are thought to date from the Bronze Age when copper ore was extracted from the sandstone. During the Roman occupation of Britain it is thought that copper ore was transported from the Edge to workshops at Wilderspool near present-day Warrington. It is unclear if the copper deposits were being worked during the Middle Ages, as there is as yet no reliable evidence for mining operations prior to 1693. Copper was mined on the Edge during the 18th century, the most intense period being between 1857 and 1877, when about 250,000 tons of ore was extracted, but the industry went into decline against competition from foreign imports.

The site of the earliest settlement at Chester had excellent facilities for the establishment of a harbour, and Chester was to become the most important port in all of northern England by the Middle Ages, through which wool, cloth and agricultural produce were exported. During the lifetime of Chester's port, one of the most important commodities that passed through the city was salt from Cheshire's famous saltworks (see page 86), a vitally important product from prehistoric times, so the silting up of the old ports along the River Dee and its estuary must have caused major difficulties for the county's salt producers. This problem may well have played a large part in the decision to canalise the River Weaver in the 18th century, in order to reach the ports along the Mersey. Subsequently, the first proper purpose-built canal, the Bridgewater Canal, was developed; such was its success that before long it had been extended to link Manchester with Runcorn. This was the beginning of the Canal Age, and soon canals were reaching almost all parts of the country, and the new industries of the Industrial Revolution quickly followed. Before long cotton mills had been established on sites all along the canals, and some of these mills are to be found in places which now seem far removed from the industrial heartlands of cities such as Manchester, in pretty little towns and villages like Marple and Bollington.

After the Second World War, the use of canals around England for the transportation of industrial goods almost completely ended. However, the boat seen on the Bridgewater Canal at Lymm in photograph L122026 is still working in the 1960s - enlargement of the photograph shows that it is carrying a cargo of coal.

BOLLINGTON, GENERAL VIEW c1955 B519006

'A thriving village with some collieries and extensive cotton factories' was how Bollington was described in 1848. Those factories were especially renowned for the quality of their Liberty cottons.

MAKING A LIVING

GRAPPENHALL, THE CANAL c1955 G200005

The Bridgewater Canal, built between 1759-76, was a key transport network of the early Industrial Revolution, linking Manchester to Runcorn and carrying freight and passengers. The towpath on the right bank was used by the horse which once pulled the barges. Grappenhall has two of the characteristic narrow hump-backed bridges designed to carry road traffic over the canal. In this area the canal was used for the transportation of fustian, a form of rough cotton known as 'poor man's velvet' that was produced locally.

LYMM, THE CANAL c1960 L122026

Runcorn became an important port in the Middle Ages, trading with Dublin in particular, but new industries began to develop in the 17th and 18th centuries, such as shipbuilding (using timber from the nearby Delamere Forest) and tanneries. This latter industry was to become extremely important with the development of factories throughout the region during the Industrial Revolution, as endless lengths of leather belting were needed for the factory machines to run smoothly. It was also around this time that Runcorn became a major producer of soap, and by 1816 there were two factories in the town producing soap and turpentine. Another, linked, industry was the production of alkali. An essential ingredient of soap, alkali was also needed in the production of glass and for the finishing of textiles in, for example, Manchester's many cotton mills. By the end of the 19th century the production of alkali was the major industry on both sides of the River Mersey, not only in Runcorn but also in Widnes, one of the new towns acquired by Cheshire in the county boundary changes of 1974.

This development came at terrible cost. The new chemical industries were not regulated at first so the air here was particularly foul, and the pollution from the chemical industries was to become the worst in the whole country. At one time the borough of Liverpool sued that of Widnes because of the damage being done by the pollution to the trees in Sefton Park. Although in the 1860s and 1870s Alkali Acts were passed to ensure stricter control of the conditions under which people worked, these had little effect. In 1888 Widnes was described as 'the dirtiest, ugliest and most depressing town in England', and in 1905 a visitor said that the town was 'a poisonous hell-town ... a dark, dreadful place of belching, poisonous fumes, defiling and degrading the brightness'. In the 21st century all has changed - the air is clean once more and the trees are flourishing, and the Widnes and Runcorn area has become an extremely sought-after place in which to live.

MAKING A LIVING

RUNCORN, THE DOCKS C1900 R67301

This view shows the docks at Weston Point. The enormous piles of white stone are actually piles of china clay from Cornwall, awaiting trans-shipment onto narrow boats so they can be taken to the china factories in Stoke-on-Trent. Later the finished article would be exported through here - in 1883 alone, 50,000 tons of china goods were exported through this port.

RUNCORN, WESTON 1929 82379

NORTHWICH, THE RIVER FROM WINNINGTON BRIDGE C1955 N43023

In the 20th century new chemical industries were developed both in the heartland of Cheshire around Northwich and Winsford and also along the coast at places such as Runcorn, including industries linked to photographic chemicals, insecticides, munitions, drugs, antiseptics and cosmetics, as well as the enormous oil refinery at Stanlow. The ICI chemical works at Winnington, Northwich, are shown in photograph N43023. A plant was established here in 1873 by John Brunner and Ludwig Mond to produce soda ash from salt. In 1926 they merged with several other companies to form the chemical giant Imperial Chemical Industries Limited (ICI).

WILMSLOW, GROVE STREET C1955 W103006

Once referred to as 'the largest village in England', Wilmslow also became an industrial centre in the 18th century. It was famous for the production of button moulding, although, as in so many towns in the area, cotton was also an important industry here.

MAKING A LIVING

In the 17th century Macclesfield was a significant town. Its position between the Cheshire Plain and the Peak District made it a busy market centre for its agricultural hinterland, and there appears to have been an important leather industry at that time. Button making also became important, in which silk or mohair thread was worked on to wooden buttons in elaborate designs. This cottage industry spread to surrounding villages, and trade connections enabled local merchants to diversify into supplying silk thread for the London market and later into other silk goods. By the last quarter of the 18th century, the town enjoyed a lucrative export trade to the American colonies, Holland and even Russia. Daniel Defoe commented on the fame of Macclesfield's buttons in his 'Complete English Tradesman', published in 1726, when he listed all the English towns which contributed to the making of a full suit of clothes:

'If his coat be of woollen-cloth, he has that from Yorkshire; the lining is shalloon from Berkshire; the waistcoat is of callamanco from Norwich; the breeches of a strong drugget from Devizes, Wiltshire; the stockings being of yarn from Westmorland; the hat is a felt from Leicester; the gloves of leather from Somersetshire; the shoes from Northampton; the buttons from Macclesfield in Cheshire, or, if they are of metal, they come from Birmingham, or Warwickshire; his garters from Manchester; his shirt of home-made linen of Lancashire, or Scotland'.

Photograph W561004 shows Winsford in central Cheshire in the early 1960s. Winsford sits on beds of almost pure salt laid down about 200 million years ago. Mining has been carried out here for centuries, and today salt is still extracted locally - it is the only working rock salt mine in Britain. The salt is used for gritting roads in icy weather or for the production of fertiliser. The salt mines

WINSFORD, THE FLASHES C1960 W561014

WINSFORD, WHARTON HILL C1955 W561004

underground are enormous, so large that miles and miles of road systems, big enough for double-decker buses, have been formed below ground to travel around on. It is no wonder that, through history, these great holes have sometimes collapsed. Some of them subsequently filled with water to become lakes, known locally as flashes.

MAKING A LIVING

Macclesfield became a major centre of the British silk industry in the 18th century. Mill Street in the town was so named because it was at the bottom of this street in 1743, by the River Bollin, that Charles Roe established his silk-throwing mill. Previously the production of silk thread had been very much a cottage industry, but Charles Roe's mill for silk-throwing used water-powered machinery, originally of Italian design but brought to England by John Lombe of Derby. Roe's mill was a success, and others soon followed, eventually using steam power rather than water. In 1765 it was estimated that in and around Macclesfield some 12,000 to 15,000 people were employed in the silk industry as a whole. Some were working in the new factories, while others still worked from home. Some of the old silk mills still survive, although now put to other uses, as do some of the silk workers' cottages, such as those in Paradise Street. Today the town proudly showcases its industrial heritage in a variety of museums ranging from the working machinery of Paradise Mill to the costume collection of the museum at the Heritage Centre, where many exhibits are made from the fabric that brought wealth to 18th- and 19th-century Macclesfield, and gave it the name of 'Silk Town'. Paradise Mill in Park Lane, which was working commercially until 1981, survives today as a museum dedicated to the silk industry, where weaving demonstrations are given on the old machinery. There are 26 restored Jacquard handlooms at the mill, which were used to make elaborately patterned cloth. First of all, the pattern had to be created on paper, which was then transferred on to a card with punched holes which outlined the design. This card fitted into the cylinder of the Jacquard machine, which controlled the various lifting arrangements of warp threads in conjunction with each throw of the weaver's shuttle. The cylinder in the Jacquard machine moved round when the weaver worked the loom by pressing on the treadle.

Although Macclesfield was famous for its silk industry, there were also cotton mills in the town and a wide variety of other industries. Macclesfield was described in the following words in the second half of the 19th century:

'The manufacture of silk, mohair, and twist buttons was formerly the chief employment; but the manufacture of all kinds of silk, including ribbons, sarcenets, gros-de-naples, satin, silk velvets, vestings, and all sorts of silk handkerchiefs, has superseded the former manufacture, and is carried on more extensively here than anywhere else in England … The manufacture of upholsterers' trimmings and similar articles is carried on in one extensive establishment; the manufacture of gimps, fringes, and other silk trimmings is carried on in numerous establishments; and the manufacture of cotton and alpaca goods was about to be introduced in 1865.'

(John Marius Wilson, 'Imperial Gazetteer of England and Wales', 1870-72)

Macclesfield Stripe was a fabric made in the town which was woven with a crepe warp and a spun silk weft. This made the material drape particularly well, but it was also extremely durable and could be washed at a very high temperature so it was ideal for making items like handkerchiefs, blouses and dresses. It was very popular in the 1920s and 1930s. The costume collection of the museum at the Heritage Centre holds examples of Macclesfield Stripe.

DID YOU KNOW?

Silk is produced from the cocoons of silkworms. The principal food-source for silkworms is the leaves of mulberry trees.

MAKING A LIVING

On 30 November 1745 a small advance party belonging to Prince Charles Edward Stuart's Jacobite army entered Macclesfield and gathered at the cross in the Market Place. They distributed leaflets and tried without success to drum up a few recruits for Prince Charles's cause. Shortly after they had left, a troop of Royal Dragoons arrived in the town, and were billeted overnight. The following morning, as the commanding officer was assuring the mayoress that he and his men would protect her, news arrived of the imminent arrival of the prince and his main army. It was said that in the panic that followed, the dragoons left town in as much haste as did the mayoress. The mayor reluctantly read an Address of Welcome to Prince Charles Edward Stuart in front of the Guildhall, and this welcome is commemorated in one of the famous woven silk pictures which were made in Macclesfield by Brocklehurst Whiston Amalgamated Ltd.

Although Macclesfield is known as 'Silk Town', Congleton actually produced the most silk of the two towns. A water-powered silk mill was built on its riverbank in the 1750s. This was only the fourth such mill in the country, and at that time it was the largest. It was 240ft long and 48ft high, but only 24ft wide, in order to make the best use of daylight (see photograph 48675, page 66).

The mill was built to house a number of machines for 'throwing' silk, preparing the unwound filaments from silkworm cocoons, and combing and twisting them into strong thread. The machinery was driven by a single waterwheel. This wheel, and the other machinery, was designed by the famous millwright and engineer James Brindley, who was in business as a millwright in Leek at about this time. The waterwheel was powered by water flowing over a weir, which was originally built to supply the town's corn mill; however, the proprietors of the silk mill bought the corn mill to secure the water rights. The waterwheel of the silk mill was eventually supplemented by one of the first steam engines in Cheshire. The mill became unsafe in the 1930s and was reduced to two storeys, and was demolished in 2002, to be replaced by housing.

The original silk mill became known as the 'Old Mill' as others were built around the town. At a stroke, these mills turned Congleton from a quiet market town with high unemployment into one of the UK's first industrial towns.

Thereafter, industry developed extensively in the town, mainly in the various branches of the textile trade, until the mid 20th century, when new industries were introduced and textiles declined.

There was a depression in the silk industry in the late 19th century, resulting in widespread unemployment amongst the silk workers of Congleton. One result of this was the introduction of the trade of 'fustian cutting', in which the looped pile of a material somewhat like corduroy was slit with a knife to produce a velvet-like fabric. This involved the worker walking the entire length of the mill, slitting one row of loops in a stretched-out piece of material with a special knife, and then walking back again, slitting the next row. It is said that a worker walked over 20 miles on a shift, and bending over the work led to a permanent stoop.

Warrington is an industrial town on the north bank of the Mersey, and was for centuries the gateway into Lancashire. Formerly in Lancashire, Warrington was ceded to Cheshire during the local government reorganisation of 1974, much to the annoyance of many of its inhabitants. Daniel Defoe visited Warrington in the 1720s and described it as 'a large, populous and well built town - rich and full of good country tradesmen'. Warrington developed and prospered as a centre for a variety of industries in the 18th

MAKING A LIVING

CONGLETON, THE OLD MILL 1902 48675

and 19th centuries, including glass-making, pin production, clock-making, tanning, sailcloth manufacture, iron and steel works, textile, soap-making and chemical industries, with brewing particularly important. By the early 20th century, Warrington could proudly claim to be 'the Town of Many Industries'. Commercial barges glided along the Bridgewater Canal, and ocean-going vessels brought raw materials along the Manchester Ship Canal and exported the products of north-western industries. Many of the town's traditional industries have now disappeared, a reflection of the national decline in manufacturing, and Warrington now promotes itself as 'The Town where Business Goes to Work'.

WARRINGTON, MANCHESTER SHIP CANAL c1960 W29088

KNUTSFORD AND CENTRAL CHESHIRE

' … for keeping the trim gardens full of choice flowers without a weed to speck them; for frightening away little boys who look wistfully at the said flowers through the railings; for rushing out at the geese that occasionally venture into the gardens if the gates are left open; for deciding all questions of literature and politics without troubling themselves with unnecessary reasons or arguments; for obtaining clear and correct knowledge of everybody's affairs in the parish; for keeping their neat maidservants in admirable order; for kindness (somewhat dictatorial) to the poor, and real tender good offices to each other whenever they are in distress, the ladies of Cranford are quite sufficient. 'A man', as one of them observed to me once, 'is so in the way in the house'.

(from 'Cranford',

Elizabeth Gaskell, 1853)

KNUTSFORD, THE COFFEE HOUSE c1955 K47018

This photograph shows the former King's Coffee House. Originally built by Richard Harding Watt in 1907 to house Knutsford's Urban District Council, it is now home to a restaurant. The tower on the top is a memorial to Elizabeth Gaskell. Born in Knutsford in 1810, Elizabeth Gaskell was to immortalise the town in her novel 'Cranford', which gives a wonderfully evocative picture of life in a small country town in the mid 1800s.

The Knutsford-born author Elizabeth Gaskell taught at the local Unitarian chapel Sunday School, and she and her husband William are buried in the chapel yard. After her marriage Mrs Gaskell and her husband went to live in Manchester, where Mr Gaskell was a Unitarian minister, and she wrote several novels sympathetically depicting the hardship of life in industrial England in the 19th century, including 'Ruth', 'Mary Barton' and the recently televised 'North and South'. She was also a great friend of Charlotte Brontë, and wrote her biography.

KNUTSFORD FROM THE AIR 1964   AFA142218

KNUTSFORD AND CENTRAL CHESHIRE

▼ Knutsford, The Rose and Crown 1898 42119

The local story is that Knutsford is named after King Canute (c994-1035), who is supposed to have forded the Lily stream here. The connection is commemorated by a mosaic of the king at Canute Place. Although the attractive Rose and Crown does not have quite such ancient origins, it is still very old, and is dated 1641.

▶ Mobberley, The Bird in Hand
c1955 M238011

The Bird in Hand stands beside the road linking Knutsford with Wilmslow. Although the sign portrays a hunting bird, there is sometimes an alternative meaning for pubs with this name. 'A bird in the hand is worth two in the bush,' goes the old saying; hence the landlord could be warning visitors that a coin in his hand is worth any number of promises - in other words no credit will be given to customers!

◀ **MOBBERLEY THE VICTORY HALL C1955 M238007**

The Victory Hall means that Mobberley's original place-name meaning 'the clearing in the forest where meetings are held' still holds true today. The hall itself was built soon after the First World War ended. Meetings of another sort take place behind the hall, where there is also a bowling green.

▶ **LOWER PEOVER, THE COBBLES AND THE CHURCH C1965 L308005**

St Oswald's Church sits right at the end of a very rough cobbled road, hence the street is called The Cobbles. This is a really beautiful church in a lovely setting with some particularly fine box pews inside. The visitor may well be very struck by the quality and preservation of the detail of the carving of so many of the tombstones in the churchyard both here and in many nearby churches.

KNUTSFORD AND CENTRAL CHESHIRE

LOWER PEOVER, THE BELLS
C1955 L308009

The main entrance to the pub is at the other side, but there is a gate giving access from the churchyard. The official name of this pub, parts of which are said to be around 700 years old, should be the Warren de Tabley Arms. The name does not refer to the church bells; instead it gets its name because in 1871 the landlord was a man called George Bell, and since then the pub has been known as the Bells. George Bell is now said to haunt the beer cellar. Incidentally, the village name is pronounced 'peever'.

GOOSTREY
THE CHURCH
C1965 G199013

St Luke's Church is pictured in the centre. The white building beside it is The Red Lion Inn; there is a sign on the tree in front of the church which says 'No Coaches'. Perhaps the village's name indicates an early link with geese, but instead today it is the home to an annual gooseberry show, which seems most apt.

Local legend says that a yew tree in St Luke's churchyard at Goostrey was used to make archers' bows during the Hundred Years' War. Cheshire's bowmen were the considered the best in the country at that time, and land at Goostrey was granted to two archers in 1365 following the Battle of Poitiers.

KNUTSFORD AND CENTRAL CHESHIRE

THE JODRELL BANK RADIO TELESCOPE c1965 C151092

In 1956 Cheshire became the home of 'Lovell's Saucer' near Goostrey, the local name for the Jodrell Bank radio telescope. It was set up by Professor Bernard Lovell, and was then the largest radio telescope in the world, at 250ft in diameter. It is accompanied now by several smaller radio telescopes. Not only is Jodrell Bank important for scientists, but today there is also a planetarium there to explain the heavens to ordinary visitors.

MIDDLEWICH, THE WHITE BEAR HOTEL c1950 M237003

Along with Northwich and Nantwich, Middlewich is one of the three salt towns of Cheshire. It sits over the old Roman town of Salinae. Salt was a very important commodity in the past, so much so that salt ('sal' in Latin) was often used as a means of payment for soldiers in the Roman army - hence our word 'salary' today. Wheelock Street, pictured here, is now a busy one-way road.

◄ WINSFORD, HIGH STREET FROM WINSFORD BRIDGE 2003
W561701

The entire heart of the town has been moved over the hill to a new site, so that the little that remains of the old High Street is now totally run down. Most, however, has been demolished to make way for a new dual carriageway through the town. The one point of reference that remains to link this photograph with No W561003 is the old post office building on the right (now painted white) and the building on the hilltop.

◄ WINSFORD
THE GENERAL POST
OFFICE C1955
W561003

The town of Winsford did not exist until the Weaver River was canalised in 1731 - this was needed to link the local salt fields with the Mersey River. In the first year of operation, goods weighing 76,000 tons were carried on the canal. Salt is still mined here from huge underground caves. John Bradbury, former Chief Cashier of the Bank of England, was born here - it was he who introduced one pound and ten shilling bank notes.

▲ WINSFORD, THE WAR MEMORIAL AND THE SCHOOLS C1955 W561011

A dual carriageway was built all along this length of road in the 1960s, but fortunately all these buildings survive. The school in the foreground dates from 1906, and beyond it are Brunner Guildhall and Verdin Grammar School, which both date from the 1890s; the latter is now used by the Mid Cheshire College. The war memorial, however, has been removed.

◄ OVER, THE SQUARE
C1965 092001

Although technically a town (it received a charter in 1280), Over never really developed, and in 1894 was recognised as 'the smallest municipality in the country.' There is a busy roundabout on this site today. Robert Nixon was born near here in the 15th century. On 22 August 1485 he fell into a trance, and afterwards said that a great battle had taken place and that there was a new king. The Battle of Bosworth had taken place that very day.

KNUTSFORD AND CENTRAL CHESHIRE

The beautiful white gates pictured here are not the ones that give this village its name - the name probably arose from much older gates at the nearby Vale Royal Abbey, once the largest Cistercian abbey in England. These gates date to 1776, and have recently been restored. The church is dedicated to St Mary; it is relatively modern, having been built in the 1870s to a design by John Douglas.

SANDIWAY, THE BLUE CAP HOTEL c1955 S490030

Hunting was a popular sport in the area for many years. When pubs were named to commemorate hunts it was usually after horses or their riders who had achieved fame. The Blue Cap, however, commemorates a famous foxhound that lived in the 1760s; this does not appear to fit with the date of 1716 that can be seen just above the entrance!

HATCHMERE, THE FOREST CAFÉ c1955 H528034

Judging by the newspaper headlines, this photograph was obviously taken on a Sunday. The Sunday Mirror advertises 'the world of the formerly married', the News of the World is telling us 'the inside story of the film, Ulysses', the People wants us to know 'the truth at last by the man who knows' (about debutantes) and the Sunday Express is shouting about '1,000 hours of hell.'

HATCHMERE, THE LAKE AND THE CAFÉ c1955 H528010

Hatchmere sits on the edge of the Delamere Forest, which now extends for some 2,400 acres. It was once a much larger hunting ground for the Earls of Chester before becoming a royal forest. James I was the last royal to hunt here when he came in the early 1600s.

◄ ACTON BRIDGE
THE RIVER WEAVER NEAR ACTON
SWING BRIDGE C1955 A235011

'Weaver' is an interesting Celtic
river name that apparently owes
its origins to Latin: it comes from
the word 'vibrare', which meant
'winding'. If this is the case, then
the name could perhaps date back
to the period of Roman occupation
in Britain.

Now used for pleasure boating, the River Weaver would once have been very busy with boats carrying salt to
ports along the Mersey estuary. As well as exporting salt, the Weaver was also used to bring coal to Winsford,
Northwich and Wilmington, and at one time china clay was also brought by barge to Winsford, where it was
trans-shipped into horse-drawn wagons and taken by road to the Potteries. There is a law (which has never been
repealed) which states that 'to swim in the River Weaver on a Sunday is an offence punishable by deportation to
the Colonies'.

◀ WEAVERHAM
HIGH STREET c1955 W368001

Weaverham straddles an old Roman road, thus reminding us of the importance of the salt mines in this area nearly 2,000 years ago. In the 1930s an excavation in the local churchyard unearthed a mass grave of 50 skeletons in which many of the skulls had a single bullet hole in the forehead - this macabre discovery was dated to the Civil War period, and was probably a mass execution. Today Weaverham is very much a suburb of Northwich to the south-east. However, thanks largely to a bypass going around the village, it still retains much of its old charm. For example, the two black and white buildings we can see at the end of the street are both still thatched.

▲ COMBERBACH, THE WAR MEMORIAL c1955 C479006

The war memorial commemorates those killed in both the First and Second World Wars. It is interesting to recall that there was a First World War prisoner of war camp in the village; it was in the grounds of Marbury Hall, which was demolished in the 1960s. Just behind the memorial the flat area of ground is a bowling green, with today a fine new clubhouse just beyond.

◀ COMBERBACH, THE AVENUE
c1955 C479001

When the prisoner of war camp closed at Marbury Hall in 1918, one of the timber huts was moved to this site to act as a garage. Amazingly, it is still there, virtually unchanged from the time of this photograph, except that the Esso sign now reads Flare and the petrol pumps have been replaced by more modern versions - although the old ones are still there at the side of the garage.

There is a pub in Comberbach with the lovely name of the Spinner and Bergamot - apparently it was named for two local racehorses. Another horse associated with Comberbach is the Marbury Dunne; but this is a ghostly one, sometimes seen with a lady in the saddle, which roams the grounds of the former Marbury Hall.

KNUTSFORD AND CENTRAL CHESHIRE

GREAT BUDWORTH
THE VILLAGE 1898 42152

When the Domesday survey was carried out in 1086, Budworth was listed as one of the largest parishes in all of England. Since the survey also listed it as having a priest, there would probably have been a wooden church here at that time (the survey only listed stone buildings, wooden buildings were ignored). Today's church of St Mary and All Saints is a stunning building, and dates from the 14th century.

GREAT BUDWORTH, SCHOOL LANE c1965 G201005

'The village of Big Budworth! You may travel England round, There is not such a village in the kingdom to be found.' Great Budworth is one of the prettiest of villages, and this must be one of the prettiest streets in it. The cobbles on the narrow lane still survive, giving the whole street the look of a chocolate box picture.

Pickmere, The Lake c1960 P272008

Unlike the recently formed flashes, Pick Mere ('the lake where pike are found') is a natural feature. It was formed as a hollow in the ground filled with melted ice at the end of the Ice Age. There were many such hollows, but most of them have long since dried out. Notice that the lake is called Pick Mere, but the village that sits beside it is Pickmere.

◄ BARNTON, THE TUNNEL AND THE CANAL c1955 B518006

This is a section of the Trent and Mersey Canal lying to the west of the village. On the other side of the village is the famous Anderton Boat Lift, which was built in 1875 by E Leader Williams. It was constructed to link this canal with the Weaver Navigation, but later fell into disrepair. In 1996 a charity, the Friends of Anderton Boat Lift, was formed to restore and run the lift.

It is said that the people of Barnton were once so poor that they could only afford to eat 'jam butties' - consequently the town came to be known as 'Jam Town'.

NORTHWICH, WITTON STREET 1903 49670

Northwich is a town that has quite literally, as well as metaphorically, been built upon salt, with thick rock salt seams and natural brine streams underlying much of the land in the region. By the middle of the 19th century the Northwich mines were producing almost 300,000 tons of salt a year. By the date of this photograph Northwich was on the tourist map, being one of the recommended excursions for visitors staying in Chester. One guide book states that 'an

interesting visit may be paid to the Marston Mine, 300ft deep, with a roof supported by huge pillars of salt … frequent subsidence of the earth, owing to the pumping out of brine, gives a singular appearance to many parts of the town'.

► **NORTHWICH**
OLD HOUSES 1903 49674

It would be a miracle if the building pictured here had survived for a further hundred years, and inevitably it has long since gone. It once stood in Winnington Lane near to the Victoria Hospital. The gateway through the iron railings on the right leads into the Verdin Park, which lies just behind.

◄ **NORTHWICH, CROOKED HOUSES 1903** 49673

Subsidence has been a constant problem in recent years for a number of buildings in Northwich - this has been the result of the underground mining of salt locally. As a result, new buildings in Northwich have to be built to withstand any possible slippage. These houses are thought to have stood on London Road, Leftwich.

► **NORTHWICH, WITTON STREET**
c1950 N43005

Witton Street is now completely pedestrianised, with a number of the buildings shown here totally restyled. Bratt & Evans, on the right, still survives, although it is now just known as Bratt's. The ground floor shop windows have long since been completely modernised. Apart from Bratt's, most of the shops along the street today are those familiar names found in every high street in the country.

One of the more spectacular effects of the subsidence caused by the mining of salt in the Northwich area involved the Witch and Barrel pub sinking into a big hole one Saturday night.

KNUTSFORD AND CENTRAL CHESHIRE

NORTHWICH, TOWN BRIDGE
1900 45422

This unusual bridge was both the first road swing bridge on floating pontoons in Britain (it was built in 1899) and then the first electrically operated swing bridge (in 1989). It was designed by Colonel J A Saner. It recently underwent restoration, including strengthening for today's far heavier traffic. This photograph shows Town Bridge just one year after it was constructed; the view is looking west towards Winnington Street. The gentleman on the left of the photograph wearing a peaked cap was the bridge operator.

NORTHWICH, THE VIADUCT 1898 42145

Built in the 1860s, the railway viaduct crosses three waterways - the old course of the River Weaver, the Weaver Navigation and the River Dane. Standing high above all three, it consists of 48 arches plus the two girder spans near the middle shown here.

HARTFORD, THE BRIDGE 1940
H323002

Notice the date, and notice, too, the newness and size of the road. This very early bypass around the southern side of Northwich crosses over the Weaver River Navigation Canal at this point. There has been an important crossing place over the River Weaver at Hartford for centuries. A ford there was used by the Roman road now known as Watling Street, which must have seen quite regular traffic with salt traders and Roman soldiers passing between the Delamere Forest and Castle, the site of the Roman fort of Condate (Northwich).

DAVENHAM, THE VILLAGE C1965 D152019

Davenham gets its name from the River Dane (a 'trickling stream'), although it sits just about halfway between it and the River Weaver. In 1965, according to a sign in the window of Price's electrical shop in the centre of the village, it was possible to rent a television at a cost of eight shillings a week. The sign is in the shop window with the blind drawn down, and can be deciphered when the photograph is considerably enlarged.

CHESHIRE'S SALT INDUSTRY

CHESHIRE'S SALT INDUSTRY is based upon salt which was laid down 255-190 million years ago, during the Triassic period, when a shallow tropical sea covered the area. Salt has always been a valuable commodity; it was used initially as a food preservative, but later for chemical and manufacturing industries. It is known that from the 1st century AD the Romans were collecting brine from naturally occurring brine springs that surfaced along the banks of the River Weaver. Salt-making was probably started during this period under military supervision, and four lead salt-pans, with cast inscriptions dating them to this period, have been found in the Northwich area. Natural brine is made when groundwater dissolves the rock salt and then flows as brine streams that sporadically erupt at the surface with very high salt concentrations. The brine can then be collected, the water evaporated off and salt crystals produced.

'Wich' is the Anglo-Saxon term for saltworks, and Cheshire's three main 'wich' towns were Northwich, Nantwich and - in the middle between them - Middlewich.

During the late Anglo-Saxon period Northwich, Middlewich and Nantwich benefited from their high status as important salt-producing centres. When the Domesday Book was compiled in 1086 the salt industry of Cheshire was considered important enough for a detailed account to be entered, including fines to be levied for the overloading of carts and packhorses.

By the time of the Domesday survey the salt industry in Northwich was well developed. The salt workers lived alongside the line of the old Roman road in Witton.

During the Middle Ages, salt, being an indispensable necessity of life, was fundamental to the prosperity of the town, and the salt-making process was highly organised and regulated. The town's motto is 'Sal est Vita' - 'Salt is Life'. In 1670, workmen prospecting for coal at nearby Marbury happened upon rock salt, a discovery that not only rocketed Northwich to the forefront of salt production and made it one of the leading forces in the Industrial Revolution, but dealt a considerable blow to the rival salt industries at Nantwich and Middlewich. Changes in the method of salt extraction occurred at this time too, with deep mining and the small lead pans being replaced by larger iron pans which could be heated by coal in order to evaporate the water quickly. After 1779, new borings revealed that even deeper saltbeds existed, and extended over a much wider area than had been previously thought. These new lower beds, at about 175ft deep, were up to 12ft thick and of exceptional quality. With the sinking of deeper mines in 1781, salt production from 23 local salt mines increased dramatically from about 15,000 tons per year in the middle of the 18th century to over 100,000 tons at its end.

The River Weaver has played an important part in the development of the salt industry in Northwich. Prior to 1721 it was a shallow waterway that flowed serenely from its source in the Peckforton Hills through the settlements of Wrenbury, Audlem, Nantwich, Winsford, Northwich and finally Frodsham before pouring into the saline waters of the River Mersey. The Weaver had been used to move salt away from Cheshire for centuries, but only along its lower tidal reaches. Salt was brought down to the river on pack-horses to meet the oncoming tide, and sailing barges would load at high water and depart for Liverpool and other ports on the ebbing tide. This was a very labour intensive and unsatisfactory method, not helped by ever changing tide heights and times; so, in 1721, an Act of Parliament was granted to make the river a navigation from Frodsham through Northwich to Winsford, some 20 miles inland. By 1723 the river had been straightened out, the channel deepened and a series of locks built that could accommodate cargo boats of 100 tons. Northwich became an inland port. When the Trent and Mersey Canal was built in 1777, the trustees of the Weaver Navigation were understandably very alarmed at the prospect of losing trade to the new waterway, but in the event the opposite occurred, and trade along the Navigation increased. At Anderton the canal and the river ran parallel to each other, with the canal being just 50ft above the river. By 1800 a physical link had been established between the two waterways, which consisted of a series of chutes; these allowed salt to be tipped from the barges on the canal into 'Weaver flats' on the river below. This system continued until 1875, when the great Anderton boat lift, known as 'the wonder of the waterways', was constructed, which raised and lowered boats between the two waterways, originally operating on a hydraulic system, and later by electricity. By contrast, the salt industry in Nantwich and Middlewich suffered as a result of the shelving of a scheme to open the rivers of those towns to navigation; consequently, salt from Nantwich and Middlewich attracted higher transport costs than that from Northwich.

By the middle of the 19th century, in addition to the a number of works producing salt by the evaporation process, the Northwich mines were producing almost 300,000 tons of salt each year. By 1887 Cheshire was producing 80% of British output, and after coal and iron, salt was the largest bulk export commodity. However, the fast-increasing output and the dangerous process of brine pumping led to large-scale subsidence throughout the saltfield. There has always been natural subsidence in the area, and several of the meres and flashes (lakes) are a result of this natural phenomenon, but the extraction of rock salt greatly accelerated the process. Cavernous holes

appeared in streets, cracks developed in roads and walls, some buildings began to tilt at crazy angles, and others simply began to sink below ground. For many years the salt companies refused to accept liability for subsidence and the immense damage it caused, but in 1891 the Brine Pumping (Compensation of Subsidence) Act was passed, and people who had suffered the consequences were able to claim compensation. Not only were buildings at risk from the salt industry, but the salt workers too. In 1838 Ashton's Mine at Witton flooded, and seven men were drowned when a rush of water through the subterranean galleries overwhelmed them before they could reach the surface.

In 1873 John Brunner and Ludwig Mond purchased the Winnington Hall estate at Northwich, where they established a plant that produced soda ash from salt. In 1926 Brunner Mond merged with other companies to form ICI, the largest salt makers in what was then the British Empire. Today, brine from the salt works is used to make a range of alkali products that are used in the glass, cosmetic, fabric, paper and pharmaceutical industries. At the beginning of the Second World War there were several salt mines in operation at Winsford. The biggest was that belonging to the Salt Union, whose facility stretched along the banks of the Weaver from Winsford to Meadow Bank, where the large evaporation pans for producing table salt were situated. The Salt Union eventually became a part of ICI, and although salt is still mined, the banks of the Weaver are lined with the remains of buildings and derelict loading staithes.

Over 250 shafts and mines have been located in and around Northwich, but the production of salt ceased in the town in 1847. For an in-depth history of salt in the Northwich area, the Salt Museum based in Weaver Hall on London Road is completely devoted to an explanation and interpretation of the salt industry, and is a must for any local or visitor to the region.

WARRINGTON AND THE NORTH OF CHESHIRE

Warrington was once famous for the sailcloth which was manufactured here, and a writer in the 1770s said that Warrington supplied 'nearly one half of the Navy of Great Britain'.

WARRINGTON, THE ACADEMY AND THE CROMWELL STATUE 1901 47251

Sitting beside the River Mersey, Warrington developed as an important junction for both road and river traffic. This photograph was taken in Bridge Foot, where the first bridge over the river here was built in the 13th century. Today there are numerous road, rail and foot bridges crossing both the river and the Ship Canal further south. The statue of Oliver Cromwell was erected in 1899 outside the Academy to mark the 300th anniversary of his birth. It was the gift of a local non-conformist Frederick Monks. The Academy building was sliced from its foundations in May 1981 and in a major feat of engineering was moved a short distance to the empty plot where the Tower Restaurant had stood, but was later demolished and rebuilt. It can be seen in its new incarnation on the opposite page.

WARRINGTON
THE ACADEMY 2003
W29701

Known as The Academy because it was home to the Warrington Academy in 1757, the building today is home to the Warrington Guardian newspaper. The statue of Oliver Cromwell now stands at the side. He appears to be pointing at the ground, and the local joke is that he is pointing at a nearby drain that needs to be cleaned.

WARRINGTON, BRIDGE STREET 2003 W29702

For many people around the world, the name 'Warrington' is associated with a dreadful atrocity when a terrorist bomb blew up causing the deaths of two young children and maiming many others one Saturday afternoon in 1993. Today the site is marked by a superb memorial to all of those affected by the tragedy. The sculpture, known as the River of Life, was designed by Stephen Broadbent, who worked on it with many local schoolchildren.

WARRINGTON AND THE NORTH OF CHESHIRE

WARRINGTON, BRIDGE STREET C1950 W29008

Just beyond Bridge Foot we enter Bridge Street. Since this photograph was taken, the lower end of the street shown here has been totally altered to make way for a new road system, so that the buildings in the foreground have now all gone.

WARRINGTON, THE CIRCUS AND SANKEY STREET C1955 W29036

Warringtonians will probably describe this photograph as Market Gate, but the title of the photograph ('The Circus') records the original concept in 1908 to create four matching corners, 'a spacious circus, perfectly symmetrical in shape with a ring of singularly graceful buildings'. Piecemeal redevelopment of Market Gate prevented realisation of this ambitious scheme. The Circus at the top of Bridge Street is now a pedestrian area. The buildings behind the bus have been totally redeveloped, and incorporate a lovely open shopping area known as Golden Square. In the Square there is a delightful sculpture of Alice in Wonderland at the Mad Hatter's Tea Party - Lewis Carroll was born in nearby Daresbury in 1832 (see page 97).

WARRINGTON AND THE NORTH OF CHESHIRE

WARRINGTON, QUEEN'S GARDENS c1955
W29047

The monument in Queen's Gardens
commemorates the Warrington soldiers of the
South Lancashire Regiment who were killed in
South Africa during the Boer War at the turn
of the 19th and 20th centuries. It was unveiled
in 1907, and Alfred Drury's bronze statue
features Lt Colonel McCarthy O'Leary; he was
killed leading the charge at Pieter's Hill which
led to the relief of Ladysmith, after shouting
'Remember men, the eyes of Lancashire are
watching you'. He is also commemorated in
the name of O'Leary Street in Warrington.

WARRINGTON, BUTTERMARKET STREET c1950 W29005

At the time these photographs were taken, Warrington
was still part of Lancashire but, after the county
boundaries were changed in the 1970s, it became part
of Cheshire. Like much of Bridge Street and the Circus
(shown here in the foreground) this street, too, is now a
smart pedestrian shopping area. The second building on
the left has a large carved pelican on the top - it was once
an inn called the Pelican.

WARRINGTON, CHURCH STREET 1894 33805

This photograph shows the Tudor cottages on the corner of Church Street with Eldon Street which popular tradition associates with the visit of Oliver Cromwell to Warrington in 1648, whilst pursuing the Scottish army. However, Cromwell did not sleep here - he actually lodged next door at the Spotted Leopard Inn, which was later the General Wolfe pub. At the time of this photograph, Mason's Stores were selling herb beer from one of these cottages.

WINWICK, THE CHURCH c1955 W370002

The church of St Oswald is one of many named for a king of Northumbria who died in the 7th century. Some claim that he was killed in battle near here when fighting against the King of Mercia, although it has to be said that Oswestry, in Shropshire, makes the same claim. The drinking fountain was erected in memory of John Thompson, who was the surveyor to the Warrington Rural District Authority between 1866 and 1900.

THELWALL, THE PICKERING ARMS C1955 T328005

Separated from the old town of Warrington by the Mersey and also (since the 1890s) by the Manchester Ship Canal, with Thelwall we are now back in that part of the county that was always Cheshire. The inscription on the pub reads 'In the Year 923 King Edward the Elder founded a city here and called it Thelwall'. Today, however, it is no longer a city in its own right, but rather a suburb of Warrington.

LYMM, THE CROSS 1897 40483

In the distance of this photograph a lone horseman rides into Lymm village as it basks in the hot sunshine which has compelled the draper, the ironmonger and Whitelegg the grocer to put up protective awnings and blinds. It is the summer of Queen Victoria's Diamond Jubilee year, but Lymm's celebrations are not complete. To commemorate the 60th anniversary of Queen Victoria's accession, the people of Lymm decided to restore the ancient cross, the centrepiece of village life. The distinguished architects Paley & Austin were commissioned to reface the worn stone steps, fix more appropriate finials and replace the cockerel with a symbolic golden crown.

LYMM
THE BRIDGEWATER
CANAL C1960 L122053

It was this canal, financed by the Duke of Bridgewater and built in 1761 by James Brindley, that was to bring about a complete change in the transportation of industrial materials and manufactured goods; it went a long way towards ensuring the success of the Industrial Revolution, which was then already under way. Notice the load of coal that is being carried in the narrow boat in the photograph. Commercial traffic ended in 1974.

WARRINGTON AND THE NORTH OF CHESHIRE

DUNHAM MASSEY
DUNHAM PARK c1885 18312

Dunham Massey is now part of Greater Manchester, although it was still in Cheshire at the time this photograph was taken. The house, and extensive grounds, are preserved by the National Trust. Although technically a Georgian house, it was extensively restyled in the early 20th century, so that it is now often described as having one of the most sumptuous Edwardian interiors of any house in the country.

HIGH LEGH, SWINYARD HALL 1897 40498

A little distance from the village of High Legh, Swinyard Hall looks much the same now as it did over one hundred years ago. Mind you, a building that looks less like a yard for swine would be hard to envisage!

DARESBURY, ALL SAINTS' CHURCH c1955 D151002

It was here in All Saints' Church that Charles Lutwidge Dodgson was baptised in 1832. But he is better known to most of us as Lewis Carroll, the author of 'Alice's Adventures in Wonderland'. Many of the characters that feature in his books are thought to have been inspired by the strange carvings within the church. Today there is a window dedicated to him in the church, with portrayals of many of his characters. Lewis Carroll had a happy boyhood here - he later wrote of Daresbury as:

'An island farm, mid seas of corn,
Swayed by the wandering
breath of morn,
The happy spot where I was born.'

WARRINGTON AND THE NORTH OF CHESHIRE

▼ Higher Walton, Walton Hall c1960 H526027

Although built in a typical Elizabethan style, this building dates to the time of the accession of Queen Victoria - it was completed in 1838. It was the home of Gilbert Greenall, who had earned his fortune as a brewer in Warrington. In 1941 the estate was sold to Warrington Corporation, and the house and a large part of the grounds is now open to the public. There is also a golf club within the grounds of the estate today.

▶ Dutton
The Village c1960
D263001

The Talbot Arms pub, the building on the right, has since been renamed the Tunnel Top. Crossing below the road at this very point there is, in fact, a tunnel for the Trent and Mersey Canal. Dutton post office, on the left, has gone, and been replaced by a new housing estate.

WARRINGTON AND THE NORTH OF CHESHIRE

◄ MOORE
THE POST OFFICE
c1950 M240004

This region was originally very marshy land near the region where the Mersey comes to the sea. When the Manchester Ship Canal was built the area was drained, and has since been used for agricultural purposes. The post office, on the left here, is now a private house. The billboards outside advertise magazines such as 'Tit Bits' and 'Men Only.' The latter apparently has a feature on 'Forces Favourites - Beautiful Colour Photos!'

► HALTON, THE CASTLE
1900 45440

Commanding an excellent viewpoint, Halton Castle was first built as a wooden castle soon after the Norman invasion of England. Before long a stone castle had replaced it, and this was to continue in use until the time of the Civil War in the 17th century, when it was besieged twice before it was finally captured. The land in the foreground has since been totally built over.

WARRINGTON AND THE NORTH OF CHESHIRE

RUNCORN, WIDNES BRIDGE
C1965 R67051

Linking Runcorn with Widnes, this bridge just gleams whenever the sun shines. Built in 1956-61 to accommodate the enormous increase in road traffic, the roadway hangs from a single steel arch, the top of which is 306ft above the high-watermark level. When it was first built it was the largest steel arch in Europe. Today it carries four lanes of traffic, having been widened in 1977.

RUNCORN, THE RAILWAY VIADUCT 1900 45434

The towers at each end of the viaduct can just be distinguished behind the bridge in photograph R67051. The viaduct was the first structure to cross the Runcorn Gap, and was built in the 1860s. At that time it also had a walkway along it, so that pedestrians could also cross the river at this point.

WARRINGTON AND THE NORTH OF CHESHIRE

RUNCORN
WESTON ROAD
1923 73913

This photograph shows the view from Runcorn Hill over the industrial area to the west. The Mersey estuary lies in the background. Traditionally the main industries of the area were connected with timber, shipbuilding and tanneries, although in the 20th century chemical industries became more important.

RUNCORN, THE LOCKS C1955 R67002

Roads, railways and also canals run through Runcorn. It is from here that the Bridgewater Canal drains to the sea. Although not part of the original canal, which opened in 1761, the section that linked up with Runcorn was built soon afterwards, and was opened in 1776.

▼ WIDNES, VICTORIA SQUARE c1965 W97078

Once again, having crossed the bridge, we are back in that area of Cheshire that was once part of Lancashire until the county boundary changes of 1974. All the buildings pictured here survive, although the general outlook has changed considerably - much of the area is now paved over to form a large open piazza.

► WIDNES, THE TECHNICAL SCHOOL AND THE PUBLIC LIBRARY 1900 45442

This is the building on the far left of picture W97078, but this time taken in an age before the motorcar was to change the look of our streets for ever. Originally constructed in 1895-96, it has recently undergone total re-modelling and refurbishment, and reopened as a new Lifelong Learning Centre.

◄ WIDNES, ST PAUL'S CHURCH 1900 45443

Built in 1883-84, St Paul's Church sits just beside Warrington's library and former Technical College. This photograph shows the church before the tower at the far end had an additional section placed on the top in 1907, as seen in photograph 59503, below.

► WIDNES, ST PAUL'S CHURCH AND THE FREE LIBRARY 1908 59503

When the library in Widnes opened in 1986 its first librarian was Miss Anne Proctor, who introduced a system of open access to books; Widnes was then in Lancashire, and its library was only the second in the county to have such facilities. This photograph also shows St Paul's Church, with its extended tower.

FARNWORTH
THE CHURCH AND THE
COTTAGE
1900 45446B

Once this was the
most important village
of many locally;
today it has itself
been surrounded by
the growing town of
Widnes. The cottage
pictured here has now
gone, to be replaced
by a brick house which
was only built in 2001.

FRODSHAM, HIGH STREET C1955 F176019

Frodsham was once an important town for stagecoaches, with a number of coaching inns such as the Bear's Paw (the stone gabled building on the left of the picture). This particular inn is said to have been so called because bear baiting used to take place nearby, although the sign was also that of the crest of the Savage family, who were lords of the manor of Frodsham.

WARRINGTON AND THE NORTH OF CHESHIRE

FRODSHAM, THE ROCK c1955 F176006

The oldest cottages in Frodsham are those on The Rock, in other words on the highest land in what was once predominantly very marshy terrain. It was on high ground such as this that the earliest settlers in the region established their homes. Frodsham sits at the northern end of a ridge that extends all the way to Shropshire.

HELSBY, THE VILLAGE AND THE HILL c1960 H326005

Helsby Hill totally dominates all views of the village that sits below. Once the site of an ancient Iron Age hill-fort, stone from here was quarried in the 19th century and used for the building of the docks at Liverpool. Some was also used when the cathedral at Chester was repaired. Today the escarpment is protected by the National Trust.

CHESHIRE FOOD AND RECIPES

Cheshire cheese is said to be Britain's oldest cheese, and is mentioned in the Domesday Book of 1086. The crumbly, nutty Cheshire Cheese was originally made in Chester but was later made throughout the county; 'real' Cheshire cheese is said to acquire its flavour from the salt marshes which once covered the region. It was said to have been the favourite cheese of Elizabeth I, and was described by the French in the following rhyme:

'Into the Cheshire cheese, dry and pink,
The long teeth of the English sink.'

The Cheshire Plain was historically a famous area for cheesemaking. For centuries, Cheshire cheese was produced on nearly every farm in the region, and the matured cheeses would then have been brought to markets in the local towns, particularly to Nantwich, where an annual cheese fair was established in 1820. The market hall seen in photograph C316011 (below) in Earle Street in Crewe was built by John Hill in 1854; intended as a cheese market, it had capacity for 2,000 tons of cheese. Production of this farm-made cheese peaked in 1907, when 600,000 hundredweight was produced locally, but the next year was to see the introduction of factory-processed cheese. Today there is only one farm left where the production of Cheshire cheese is totally bound to one farm, all the way from the breeding of the cows for the right milk to the maturing of the final cheese - and it is not even in Cheshire, but just over the border in Shropshire, although technically at least it is still in the Cheshire Plain region!

CHESHIRE CHEESE SOUP

600ml/1 pint good stock
275g/10oz peeled and diced potatoes
2 leeks, washed and trimmed
2 carrots, peeled and finely chopped or grated
25g/1oz oatmeal
115g/4oz grated Cheshire cheese
Salt and pepper

(Serves 4)

Put the stock into a large pan, add the vegetables and seasoning and bring to the boil. Simmer for 15 minutes, then add the oatmeal and simmer for a further 10 minutes. Just before serving, add half the cheese and stir until melted, then pour the soup into serving bowls and sprinkle the remaining cheese on top.

CREWE, THE MARKET HALL, EARLE STREET
c1951 C316011

CHESTER POTTED CHEESE

This is a good way of using up leftover pieces of cheese, as several varieties can be grated and mixed together in this recipe. It makes a tasty spread for toast.

225g/8oz grated cheese
50g/2oz butter
¼ teaspoonful ground mace or allspice
2 tablespoonfuls sweet sherry or Madeira wine
Melted butter, to seal the surface

Mix the grated cheese with the softened butter and spice - adjust the amount of butter depending on how dry or moist the cheese is that is used. Beat well, then add the sherry or Madeira and mix well again. Put the mixture into small pots or ramekins, pressing it down well. Smooth the tops, then cover each pot with melted butter. The potted cheese should be stored in the fridge, and will keep well for several weeks as long as the seal is not broken.

CHESTER PUDDING

There are two Chester pudding recipes: the oldest is a steamed suet pudding with the addition of blackcurrant jam. The recipe given below is for the second, more recent, Chester Pudding, which is rather like a Bakewell Tart but with a meringue topping.

175g/6oz shortcrust pastry
110g/4oz caster sugar
50g/2oz butter
25g/1oz ground almonds
3 eggs, separated
1 tablespoonful caster sugar for the meringue
Milk for glazing

Preheat oven to 190 degrees C/375 degrees F/Gas Mark 5.

Roll the pastry out very thinly, line a baking tin with it and brush the edges of the pastry with a little milk.
   Carefully melt the sugar and butter in a heavy saucepan, and add the ground almonds. Allow the mixture to cool slightly, then stir in the three eggs yolks and one egg white. Gently cook the mixture over a low heat, stirring constantly, until it thickens, then pour it into the pastry-lined baking tin. Bake for 20 minutes.
   When the pastry and pudding filling is cooked, remove from the oven. Whisk the remaining two egg whites until stiff, then fold in the extra tablespoonful of sugar. Spread the meringue mixture on top of the pudding. Reduce the heat of the oven to 170 degrees C/325 degrees F/Gas Mark Gas 3, and bake the pudding for about 20 minutes, or until the meringue is firm and golden on the peaks. Serve hot or cold.

CHESHIRE FOOD AND RECIPES

In 'Glimpses of Macclesfield in Ye Olden Days' (1883) Isaac Finney makes the following comment: 'Another old custom we may not omit to notice, which was formerly practised in Macclesfield, previously noting that at that time oatcake, as an article of diet, was in more general use than now. On entering almost any house of the operatives, and indeed most of the upper classes of that time, you would have observed suspended from the ceiling of the kitchen a large open frame of wood, interlaced from all points with a network of cord, called an oatcake rack, on which were spread the week's supply of oatcakes, and which were reached down or pieces broken off as required for use, when a little treacle or butter was spread upon it and eaten, hard as it was, with a relish that few now-a-days would like to submit to'.

MACCLESFIELD, PARK GREEN 1897 40442

Parkin was traditionally eaten on Bonfire Night (or Guy Fawkes' Night) on 5 November, but its older tradition is associated with the feast days marking the beginning of winter, around the time of All Saints' (or All Hallow's) Day on 1 November, and All Souls' Day on 2 November. These Christian feast days themselves have origins in the ancient Celtic feast of the dead called Samhain. In many parts of the north of England, parkin came to be called 'Harcake' or 'Soul Hars Cake', and would be offered to visitors on All Saints' Day.

CHESHIRE PARKIN

225g/8oz coarse oatmeal
75g/3oz plain flour
50g/2oz brown sugar
1 teaspoonful ground ginger
½ teaspoonful bicarbonate of soda
A pinch of salt
225g/8oz golden syrup or black treacle
125g/4oz margarine
70ml/2½fl oz milk

Preheat the oven to 180 degrees C/350 degrees F/Gas Mark 4.

Mix the dry ingredients together. Melt the syrup or treacle and margarine in a pan and add to the dry ingredients, and stir in the milk to make a soft consistency. Grease a 20cm/7-8 inch square tin and line it with greased greaseproof paper. Pour in the mixture, and bake in the middle of the preheated oven for about 1¼ hours, when the parkin should be firm to the touch. Leave in the tin to cool. This is best kept in an airtight tin for 2 days before eating.

CHESHIRE ONION PIE

175g/6oz shortcrust pastry
50g/2oz butter
450g/1lb peeled and sliced onions
25g/1oz plain flour
1 level teaspoonful salt
A good quantity of freshly ground black pepper
Freshly grated nutmeg
150ml/5fl oz single cream
1 large egg

Preheat the oven to 200 degrees C/400 degrees F/Gas Mark 6.

Roll out the pastry on a floured surface and use it to line a 20cm/7-8 inch flan dish or tin. Line the base of the pie with greaseproof paper and fill with baking beans, and bake blind in the preheated oven for 10 minutes, then remove the paper and cook for a further 5 minutes to dry out the base.

Melt the butter in a saucepan, add the onions and cook gently until soft, for about 15 minutes. Do not let them brown. Add the flour and stir in, then add the salt and pepper and freshly ground nutmeg. Gradually stir in the milk, bring to the boil and cook for 2 minutes, stirring, until thickened. Remove from the heat.

Beat the egg lightly, spoon into it a little mixture from the pan and stir in, then add to the mixture in the pan and stir in. Taste for seasoning and adjust if necessary. Spoon the mixture into the flan case, level and grate a little more nutmeg on top. Bake in the preheated oven for about 45 minutes.

For many years the Warrington area was famous for the quality of the gooseberries that were grown here, and central Cheshire has a long tradition of gooseberry-showing. The largest gooseberry ever recorded was exhibited at the Marton Village Show in Congleton in 1933; grown by Kelvin Archer, it was a Montrose Berry which weighed 39 pennyweights and 9 grains (61.9g - just over 2oz).

GOOSEBERRY AND ELDERFLOWER CREAM

500g/1½lb gooseberries
30ml/2 tablespoonfuls elderflower cordial
300ml/10fl oz double cream
115g/4oz icing sugar

Place the gooseberries in a heavy saucepan, cover and cook over a low heat, shaking the pan occasionally until they are tender. Tip the gooseberries into a bowl, crush them with a heavy wooden spoon or potato masher, then leave them to cool completely. (The gooseberries can be sieved or puréed if a finer consistency is preferred.)

Beat the cream until soft peaks form, then fold in half the crushed gooseberries. Sweeten with icing sugar to taste, and fold in the elderflower cordial. Sweeten the remaining gooseberries with icing sugar to taste.

Put a layer of the cream mixture in four dessert dishes or tall glasses, and then a layer of crushed gooseberries, then cover and chill for at least one hour before serving.

MACCLESFIELD AND THE EAST OF CHESHIRE

Although Macclesfield is famously known as 'Silk Town', it has also been known by another nickname - 'Treacle Town'. Local tradition says that this derives from an incident when a merchant spilt a quantity of treacle on Hibel Road, which the local people were quick to salvage, although another explanation says that it dates from when some mill-owners in the town provided barrels of treacle to unemployed weavers.

MACCLESFIELD, THE MARKET PLACE c1955 M2018

The imposing building on the right, now looking quite spruce and clean, is Macclesfield's Town Hall. The town's wealth was founded on its silk industry, which was largely a cottage-run industry, although there was a mill here as early as 1743. One of the mills, Paradise Mill, which was working until 1981, survives today as a museum dedicated to the industry.

MACCLESFIELD AND THE EAST OF CHESHIRE

MACCLESFIELD, CHURCHWALL GATE c1955 M2003

This view has changed little, although the pub's black and white walls have been painted over. The church beyond is St Michael's, rebuilt in 1901 to the design of Sir Arthur Blomfield, who was also the architect of the Bank of England in London. A memorial in the church recalls John Brownswood - he was headmaster of Macclesfield Grammar School, but he had also taught at Stratford Grammar School when a young Will Shakespeare was a student.

MACCLESFIELD AND THE EAST OF CHESHIRE

MACCLESFIELD
THE 108 STEPS C1955 M2002

In the Savage chapel of the church of St Michael and All Angels at Macclesfield is the tomb of the 8th John Savage and his first wife, with a Latin inscription dated 1597. The tomb is particularly interesting in that John's wife, Elizabeth Manners, daughter of the Earl of Rutland, lies higher than her husband because of her more noble birth.

MACCLESFIELD, CHESTERGATE 1898 42600

Macclesfield by 1850 was an overcrowded, filthy, lively, inventive mill town. It was the centre of the silk trade, full of little terraced cottages and clacking mills. However, the town had grown so fast that social provision, education and the basic necessities of life were all lacking for many people. The first vicar of the new St Paul's Church on Brook Street was Henry Briant. He was so distressed by the hordes of street children roaming his parish that he collected one hundred or so in a dilapidated building opposite the church; here they could be fed, sheltered, taught to read and write, and in due course be given the skills to earn their living. Eventually in 1866 a new building called the Industrial School, or more popularly the Ragged School, was constructed. It still stands on Brook Street, and its size is an astonishing testimony to the size of the problem.

MACCLESFIELD AND THE EAST OF CHESHIRE

Macclesfield was the birthplace of Hovis bread, famous for the advertising slogan of 'Don't say brown, say Hovis'. Hovis bread is made from a flour that is especially rich in wheatgerm, which was patented in 1899 by Richard Smith; the brand was developed by S Fitton & Sons Ltd, whose mill operated on the banks of the Macclesfield Canal. The name 'Hovis' was invented by a London student, Herbert Grimes, who was inspired by the Latin phrase 'hominis vis' ('the strength of man'), after Fittons set a national competition to find a trading name for the bread made from their patented flour. Fittons milled the flour and sold it to bakers with specially branded baking tins. Fittons became Hovis Ltd in 1918, and after a succession of mergers became part of Rank Hovis McDougall in 1962. The company is now part of the food conglomerate RHM, but the Hovis side of the business still specialises in high wheatgerm wholemeal flour. The former Hovis warehouse by the Macclesfield Canal is now a development of apartments.

HENBURY, THE CHURCH
1897 40467

So many of our churches around the country were rebuilt during Victorian times, and Henbury's church is no exception. St Thomas's dates from the 1840s, and was designed by Richard Lane. In view of the relatively young age of the church when this photograph was taken, it is surprising to see so much ivy climbing up the walls. This has now been removed.

CAPESTHORNE HALL
1897 40469

Set in 1,000 acres of parkland, the Jacobean-style hall dates from 1719. Following a fire it was rebuilt (in much the same style) in 1861. Still privately owned, it is opened to the public in the summer months and can also be hired for private events.

MACCLESFIELD AND THE EAST OF CHESHIRE

▼ NETHER ALDERLEY, THE CHURCH AND THE RECTORY 1896 37474

St Mary's Church sits at the end of a little lane off the A34. A 14th-century building, it has a strange pew perched up on the wall 'like an opera box'. It also has two rather precious books. One is a Breeches Bible that dates from 1560. Breeches Bibles were so named because the story of Adam and Eve covering themselves with fig leaves was translated as 'They sewed fig leaves and made themselves breeches'.

► ALDERLEY EDGE
A COPPER MINE 1896 37480

Copper (and also, to a lesser degree, lead) have been mined here since Roman times, so that the whole area of hillside behind the town is said to have dozens of pits, caves and tunnels. One mine, opened in 1857, produced 4,000 tonnes of copper before it was exhausted only twenty years later. Today this area is covered in woodland, and has become a popular spot for walkers.

◄ ALDERLEY EDGE
LONDON ROAD C1965
A29047

The town developed in the 19th century as a suburb of Manchester for those who could afford to live away from the smoke and grime, and could also spare the time to travel. Today it is still one of the best areas in which to live locally, with extremely expensive and beautiful houses owned by the wealthier element of Manchester's work force - including, at one time, David Beckham.

► ALDERLEY EDGE
CHORLEY HALL 1896 37470

Dating from long before the time when Manchester's workers even considered the need to escape to live in more peaceful and cleaner areas, Chorley Hall is thought to be amongst the oldest inhabited timber-framed houses in the county. It dates from the 1300s, and is still being altered to suit the changing needs and fashions of today.

ADVERTISER
AND
EVENING ECHO
OFFICE FOR
ADVERTISEMENTS
FOREIGN AND ENGLISH TOYS
AND FANCY GOODS
BOOKSELLER, BOOKBINDER
GUARDIAN OFFICE

WILMSLOW
GROVE STREET
1897 39604

Like Macclesfield and
many other small towns
around, Wilmslow was
to develop enormously
in the 18th century
with the introduction of
industries linked to local
silk and cotton mills.
Today evidence of this
industrial past has all
but disappeared, with
the dominance, instead,
of plush new shops.
The shop on the corner,
W Hughes, advertises
'Foreign and English Toys
and Fancy Goods', while
a newspaper in front
announces 'Assassination
- Spanish Premier'.

WILMSLOW FROM THE AIR 1955 AFR24909

▲ Wilmslow, Grove Street 2003 W103701

Grove Street is now pedestrianised, and the buildings have changed so drastically that it is almost impossible to fit photograph 39604 (pages 116-117) to the present view of the street. Despite considerable alteration, there are parts of the building on the left that still survive, including some of the decorative detail.

◄ Wilmslow
The Memorial Gardens
c1955 W103003

The memorial gardens in the foreground remember those who died in both World Wars. Behind them is St Bartholomew's Church. Some of it probably dates from the 15th century, although it was altered considerably in the following century and again in Victorian times.

◀ STYAL, THE UNITARIAN CHAPEL 1897 39618

Today the name Styal is synonymous for most people with the National Trust, as it is also the home of the wonderful working cotton mill museum run by the Trust at Quarry Bank Mill. Perhaps because of this association, the village itself also remains very unspoilt.

▶ STYAL, THE COTTON MILL 1897 39616

The cotton mill at Styal was established by Samuel Greg in 1784; its location on the bank of the fast-flowing River Bollin meant that the mill could be water-powered without extensive engineering. Like many mill owners of his day, Greg employed children in his mill, to piece the threads and keep the machinery clean. The readiest source of child labour was pauper apprentices, and in 1793 the Apprentice House was built near the mill to house them.

◀ HANDFORTH, POST OFFICE PARADE c1965 H322021

Although Handforth is very much busier these days, this view has changed little, and only in the detail. Technically, the boundary between the conurbation of Greater Manchester and the county of Cheshire lies just to the north of Handforth, but in reality this is very much an extension of that great city.

HOCKLEY
COPPICE ROAD AND
THE POST OFFICE
C1960 H367011

Today the little village of
Hockley has been absorbed
by nearby Poynton. Although
just within the county of
Cheshire, this area has now, like
Handforth to the west, become
more of a suburb of Manchester.
It still retains a countryside feel,
however, although new buildings
are rapidly encroaching upon it.

CHESHIRE FOLKLORE, SAYINGS AND CUSTOMS

Although immortalised by Lewis Carroll in 'Alice's Adventures in Wonderland', the origins of the Cheshire Cat are said to go way back in time, and no one really knows where the story of the grinning cat, now always associated with Cheshire, first came from. One theory is that it originates from a carving of a cat on the tower of St Wilfrid's Church at Grappenhall, but another is that it comes from the custom of making early Cheshire cheeses in an oval shape, which resembled a curled-up cat. But the Cheshire cat may not even be a cat at all - another interpretation of the story is that it may derive from the arms of Hugh, the first Earl of Chester, who was nicknamed 'Lupus', or 'the Wolf', because of his ferocity; his coat of arms depicted the snarling face of a wolf, which may have been mistaken for a grinning cat.

There are several old sayings linked with Chester. 'There's more than one yew-bow in Chester' was a saying used to console broken-hearted girls who had been spurned by their lovers. It is believed to have been current since the days of the Hundred Years' War, when local longbow archers helped to win the battles of Crécy, Poitiers and Agincourt. Another saying comes from an old ballad which tells how the daughter of a medieval mayor of Chester was betrothed by her father to Lord Luke de Taney, instead of the Welsh knight who she loved. During a ball game with de Taney and some friends near the city wall, she threw the ball over the wall and persuaded de Taney to search for it. While he was doing this, she slipped through the tiny Pepper Gate in the wall and escaped with her lover. Her furious father ordered the Pepper Gate to be locked in future, giving rise to the local saying: 'When the daughter is stolen, shut the Pepper Gate'. Happily, local tradition also says that father and daughter were later reconciled and the Pepper Gate was reopened.

In the south-east corner of Chester's city walls are the six short flights of stone stairs known as the Wishing Steps. They were built in 1785 and, according to tradition, your wish will be fulfilled if you can run to the top, back to the bottom and then up again without drawing breath. A similar tradition is linked with the 108 Steps in Macclesfield (see photograph M2002 on page 112), Macclesfield's best-known and steepest thoroughfare, which links Waters Green below with the Market Place above. A local tradition says that if you can run up the 108 Steps in one breath, you will gain your heart's desire.

NANTWICH, THE CHESHIRE CAT c1965 N3036

FARNDON, ST CHAD'S CHURCH C1960 F161002

St Chad's Church in Farndon is one of the few places where a rush-bearing ceremony is still carried out each year: fresh rushes are brought into the church, and also laid on the paths and graves outside. This recalls a time when churches still had mud floors which would have been covered with rushes to provide a dry footing for the congregation.

The people of Congleton have always had an affection for their local 'mountain', The Cloud. Its heather-clad top was always a popular walk from the town, even before it was acquired by the National Trust in the 1930s. It is an old tradition for Congleton people to climb The Cloud for a dawn service on Easter Day.

One of the highlights in Warrington's annual calendar is the Walking Day, a parade of groups from all the churches in the town, which is held on the closest Friday to the last day of June. The Walking Days of Lancashire and Cheshire originate from the Sunday School movement, and were an effort to free the working children of the industrial towns for a day of fun and recreation. By the 1850s Warrington Walking Day had become an annual holiday for the young people of the town. On Walking Day, children from the different church schools in Warrington would walk in a procession to the parish church, where they would hear a service and then retire for refreshments. By 1908 groups from all the different religious denominations in the town had joined in the custom, although they did not all follow the same route. Despite calls for the church groups to walk together, this only happened after the terrorist attack on Warrington in 1993.

Another popular annual event in Cheshire is Royal May Day in Knutsford, which dates back to the 1860s, and which includes the unusual tradition of 'sanding' the streets. The Royal May Day procession is led by the Green Man, otherwise known as Jack in the Green - an interesting modern sculpture of this character from medieval folklore stands outside Knutsford's Heritage Centre. 'Sanding' the streets is the custom of decorating the town's pavements with mottos and patterns made from coloured sand, and it is said to derive from the time of King Canute, after whom the town is traditionally said to have been named; apparently the king once congratulated a newly married couple at their wedding by wishing them as many children as grains of sand. At one time sanding was a wedding custom rather than a May Day event.

The Cross in Chester is where the famous medieval Mystery Plays were performed. They were a series of dramatic stories drawn from the Bible, from the Creation to the Last Judgement, including the life of Christ from birth to crucifixion and resurrection, and were first enacted by medieval craftsmen and guildsmen in the 14th century. Different guild companies were responsible for performing an individual story within the cycle of the Plays; for example, the Tanners performed The Fall of Lucifer, the Vintners performed The Three Kings, and the Tailors performed The Ascension.

The plays were revived in 1951 and have since been performed every five years; the next Mystery Plays will be performed in the summer of 2008. Chester's Mystery Plays remain a valued part of the city's cultural heritage, and attract people from all over the world.

▼ HOCKLEY, THE CANAL AT HIGHER POYNTON c1960 H367003

Completed in 1831, the Macclesfield Canal was one of the last canals to be built in England. It is also one of the highest navigable waterways in Britain, rising to over 500ft above sea level. Its route was surveyed by Thomas Telford, famous for his canals, roads and bridges all around the country. Telford died in 1834 and is buried in Westminster Abbey.

▶ DISLEY, MARKET STREET
c1960 D154003

Right in the far north-eastern corner of the county, Disley straddles the busy A6. In fact, Disley has always been a roadside settlement: its existence goes back to a time when a Roman road came through here. The town also sits on the northern boundaries of the Peak District National Park and beside the estate at Lyme Park (perhaps best known these days for the lake Mr Darcy dived into in the BBC TV version of 'Pride and Prejudice').

◄ POTT SHRIGLEY THE VILLAGE AND THE CHURCH c1955 P395025

Through the trees on the right (although almost completely hidden now) the tower of St Christopher's Church can be seen. The church was once home to what must have been one of the earliest lending libraries in England: in 1492 Geoffrey Downes left his books to the church, with specific instructions that gentlemen should be allowed to borrow them for up to thirteen weeks at a time.

► PRESTBURY, OLD COTTAGES c1950 P111015

In the middle of this collection of buildings is a pub called the Admiral Rodney. Lord Rodney, who died in 1792, is particularly remembered for his victory at the Battle of the Saintes in the West Indies, which led to peace terms with the French (for a time!). He also, it must be said, made a fortune from the slave trade, both for himself and for the city of Liverpool, where there is a street named after him.

PRESTBURY, RED HOUSE 1896 37440

This wonderful timber-framed building dates from the 1400s. It sits opposite the church, and was once the vicarage - it was known originally as the Priest's House. Today it is home to a branch of the National Westminster Bank. There has been a tradition in the village (which started as long ago as 1577) that a curfew bell should be rung at 8pm each evening during autumn and winter.

BOLLINGTON
C1955 B519003

The tall chimneys pictured here remind us of Bollington's industrial history. There were once thirteen cotton mills here, and the town was linked by both canal and rail to other industrial centres all around. The last of the cotton mills, the Adelphi, was closed in 1974, although by that time it was being used for the processing of artificial fibres rather than cotton.

BOLLINGTON, PALMERSTON STREET C1955 B519011

From being only a small village, Bollington expanded enormously in the 19th century. This expansion is reflected in a number of the streets named for famous men of that time - for example Lord Palmerston, the Duke of Wellington and Prince Albert are all remembered in this way.

MACCLESFIELD AND THE EAST OF CHESHIRE

All those cotton mills needed spun cotton, and this village, sitting right on the edge of the Peak District National Park, was once an important spinning centre. It seems far removed from any industrial activity now, and is probably once again a place for ravens - apparently the name Rainow means 'the hill frequented by ravens'.

Now a truly lovely private home, this would have been an extremely grand post office for such a remote village. In fact it is not difficult to believe that it was at one time the largest sub-post office building in the country. It began life in 1770, however, as an administrative building for a mill.

◀ GAWSWORTH
THE OLD CROSS
1897 40466

Gawsworth is an interesting name in England - the first element comes from the Welsh word 'gof' meaning a smith or smithy. So we evidently have here a reminder of an early community with both Welsh and English living together. This is something that must have happened all over the country to a greater or lesser degree, but is seldom reflected in our village place-names.

▶ GAWSWORTH
THE OLD HALL 2003
G5701

'To see Cheshire you must see Gawsworth'. Many people visit this beautiful house each year, not only because it is a stunning building, but because it has also become the venue for an annual summer season of open-air theatre and concerts. Tradition has it that the Dark Lady of Shakespeare's sonnets was Mary Fitton, who once lived here.

MACCLESFIELD AND THE EAST OF CHESHIRE

GAWSWORTH, THE VILLAGE c1960 G5021

The people of Gawsworth are very proud of an 18th-century occupant of the village. His name was Samuel 'Maggoty' Johnson, and he was the last professional jester in England. He died in 1773, and there is a lane nearby bearing his name where his grave can be found. He was also mentioned by Henry Fielding in his novel 'Tom Jones'.

GAWSWORTH, THE NEW HALL 1898 42609

Gawsworth New Hall was begun in 1707 by Lord Mohun. He was later to die in 1712 as a result of a duel with the Duke of Hamilton. The two men were fighting over the Gawsworth estate, but it did not do either of them any good - both men were killed in the duel.

GAWSWORTH
THE NEW HALL
c1960 G5106

The beautiful old trees have gone, but fortunately, as we can see from this photograph, new ones were planted; now, some forty years later, these are growing into fine replacements.

MARTON, THE CHURCH OF ST JAMES AND ST PAUL 1897 40468

Despite the brickwork at the east end, Marton's church of St James and St Paul is one of the oldest surviving timber churches in Europe - it was founded in 1343 by Sir John de Davenport, and hence the pub across the road is called the Davenport Arms. Internally the church is quite delightful, and it even has the remnants of an early medieval wall painting on the west wall.

MACCLESFIELD AND THE EAST OF CHESHIRE

▼ CONGLETON, THE LION AND SWAN HOTEL 1898 42156

The two oldest buildings in Congleton are both inns, the White Lion near the Town Hall, and the Lion and Swan, shown here.

▶ CONGLETON, ST PETER'S CHURCH 1898 42157

The original parish church was St Mary's at Astbury, but the building of this one in the 1740s reflected the growth of importance of Congleton as a result of its silk industry at that period. The stone tower was added some forty years later. The cobbles on the road in the foreground have gone, and the trees have grown more, but otherwise this view is little changed.

CONGLETON, THE TOWN HALL AND THE HIGH STREET c1955 C151034

The Town Hall is the tall building with the clock tower seen in the centre of the photograph; it was built in 1864 by E W Godwin at a cost of £8,000. The height of the building has changed since this photograph was taken - in 1967 dry rot was discovered, and in the course of repairs, the spire at the top was reduced by one foot.

Congleton, Lawton Street 1898 42154

Congleton is sometimes known as Bear Town. Bear-baiting was once so popular here that when the town's bear died just before the annual Wakes, the local people were so anxious to replace it so that the celebrations would not be spoiled that the Congleton Corporation used the money that had been set aside to buy a new Bible for the parish church to buy a new bear for 16 shillings (80p). The story is recalled in the bear that appears on the town crest.

TIMBERSBROOK, WEATHERCOCK LANE C1950 T219011

Although taken only around sixty years ago, a photograph such as this is very evocative of a world that has totally disappeared. Except for the telegraph pole on the left, this picture could have been taken at any time in the hundreds of years prior to 1950. Today it would be very rarely that you would see a horse-drawn cart here.

Acton 50
Acton Bridge 78
Alderley Edge 38, 114-115
Alsager 58
Barnton 82
Beeston 43
Birkenhead 33, 34
Bollington 60, 129
Bunbury 54, 55
Burton 31, 32
Capesthorne Hall 113
Chester 16-17, 18, 19, 20-21, 22-23, 40, 41
Cholmondeley 53
Church Minshull 56, 57
Comberbach 79
Congleton 58-59, 66, 134-135, 136-137
Crewe 44-45, 46, 47, 106
Daresbury 97
Davenham 85
Disley 126
Dunham Massey 96
Dutton 98
Eccleston 24, 25
Egremont 36
Ellesmere Port 27, 28
Farndon 125
Farnworth 104
Frodsham 40, 104, 105
Gawsworth 130-131, 132, 133
Goostrey 72

Grappenhall 61
Great Budworth 80
Hale 109
Halton 99
Handforth 121
Hartford 85
Haslington 47
Hatchmere 77
Helsby 105
Henbury 113
High Legh 96
Higher Walton 98
Hockley 122-123, 126
Hooton 26
Jodrell Bank 73
Knutsford 67, 68-69, 70
Little Budworth 56
Little Moreton Hall 59
Little Sutton 26
Lower Peover 43, 71, 72
Lymm 61, 93, 94-95
Macclesfield 12, 42, 108, 110, 111, 112
Malpas 52-53
Marbury 15, 51
Marton 133
Middlewich 73
Mobberley 70-71
Moore 98-99
Nantwich 48, 49, 124
Neston 29, 30
Nether Alderley 114
New Brighton 35, 36

Northwich 62, 82, 83, 84
Over 75
Parkgate 30, 31
Pickmere 81
Pott Shrigley 126-127
Prestbury 43, 127, 128
Rainow 14, 130
Rowton 24
Runcorn 62, 100, 101
Sandbach 42, 57, 58
Sandiway 76
Shotwick 32
Styal 121
Tarporley 55
Thelwall 93
Timbersbrook 38, 138
Wallasey 37
Warrington 66, 88, 89, 90, 91, 92
Weaverham 78-79
Whitegate 76
Widnes 102-103
Wildboarclough 130
Willaston 29
Wilmslow ... 39, 62, 116-117, 118-119, 120
Winsford 63, 74, 75
Winwick 92
Wrenbury 50, 51

FRITH PRODUCTS & SERVICES

Francis Frith would doubtless be pleased to know that the pioneering publishing venture he started in 1860 still continues today. Over a hundred and forty years later, The Francis Frith Collection continues in the same innovative tradition and is now one of the foremost publishers of vintage photographs in the world. Some of the current activities include:

INTERIOR DECORATION

Today Frith's photographs can be seen framed and as giant wall murals in thousands of pubs, restaurants, hotels, banks, retail stores and other public buildings throughout the country. In every case they enhance the unique local atmosphere of the places they depict and provide reminders of gentler days in an increasingly busy and frenetic world.

PRODUCT PROMOTIONS

Frith products are used by many major companies to promote the sales of their own products or to reinforce their own history and heritage. Frith promotions have been used by Hovis bread, Courage beers, Scots Porage Oats, Colman's mustard, Cadbury's foods, Mellow Birds coffee, Dunhill pipe tobacco, Guinness, and Bulmer's Cider.

GENEALOGY AND FAMILY HISTORY

As the interest in family history and roots grows world-wide, more and more people are turning to Frith's photographs of Great Britain for images of the towns, villages and streets where their ancestors lived; and, of course, photographs of the churches and chapels where their ancestors were christened, married and buried are an essential part of every genealogy tree and family album.

FRITH PRODUCTS

All Frith photographs are available Framed or just as Mounted Prints and unmounted versions. These may be ordered from the address below. Other products available are - Calendars, Jigsaws, Canvas Prints, Mugs, Tea Towels, Tableware and local and prestige books.

THE INTERNET

Over several hundred thousand Frith photographs can be viewed and purchased on the internet through the Frith websites!

For more detailed information on Frith products, look at
www.francisfrith.com

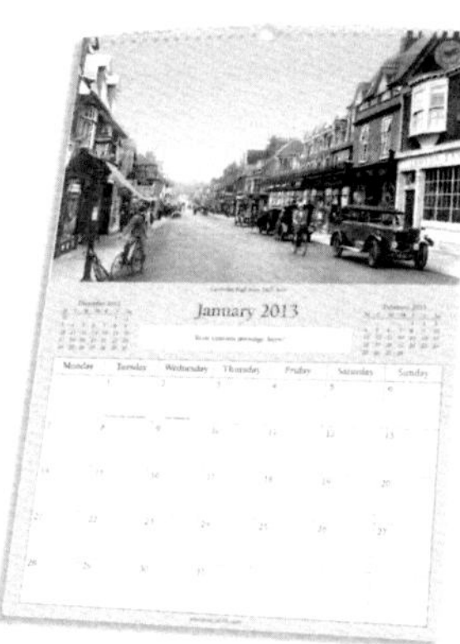

See the complete list of Frith Books at: www.francisfrith.com
This web site is regularly updated with the latest list of publications from The Francis Frith Collection. If you wish to buy books relating to another part of the country that your local bookshop does not stock, you may purchase on-line.

For further information, trade, or author enquiries please contact us at the address below:
The Francis Frith Collection, Unit 19 Kingsmead Business Park, Gillingham, Dorset SP8 5FB.
Tel: +44 (0)1722 716 376   Email: sales@francisfrith.co.uk

See Frith products on the internet at www.francisfrith.com

FREE PRINT OF YOUR CHOICE
CHOOSE A PHOTOGRAPH FROM THIS BOOK

+ POSTAGE

Mounted Print
Overall size 14 x 11 inches (355 x 280mm)

TO RECEIVE YOUR FREE PRINT

Choose any Frith photograph in this book

Simply complete the Voucher opposite and return it with your payment (to cover postage and handling) and we will print the photograph of your choice in SEPIA (size 11 x 8 inches) and supply it in a cream mount ready to frame (overall size 14 x 11 inches).

Order additional Mounted Prints at HALF PRICE - £19.00 each (normally £38.00)

If you would like to order more Frith prints from this book, possibly as gifts for friends and family, you can buy them at half price (with no additional postage costs).

Have your Mounted Prints framed

For an extra £20.00 per print you can have your mounted print(s) framed in an elegant polished wood and gilt moulding, overall size 16 x 13 inches (no additional postage required).

IMPORTANT!

❶ Please note: aerial photographs and photographs with a reference number starting with a "Z" are not Frith photographs and cannot be supplied under this offer.

❷ Offer valid for delivery to one UK address only.

❸ These special prices are only available if you use this form to order. You must use the ORIGINAL VOUCHER on this page (no copies permitted). We can only despatch to one UK address.

❹ This offer cannot be combined with any other offer.

As a customer your name & address will be stored by Frith but not sold or rented to third parties. Your data will be used for the purpose of this promotion only.

Send completed Voucher form to:

The Francis Frith Collection,

1 Chilmark Estate House, Chilmark, Salisbury, Wiltshire SP3 5DU

Voucher for **FREE** and Reduced Price *Frith Prints*

Please do not photocopy this voucher. Only the original is valid, so please fill it in, cut it out and return it to us with your order.

Picture ref no	Page no	Qty	Mounted @ £19.00	Framed + £20.00	Total Cost £
		1	Free of charge*	£	£
			£19.00	£	£
			£19.00	£	£
			£19.00	£	£
			£19.00	£	£
			£19.00	£	£

Please allow 28 days for delivery.
Offer available to one UK address only

* Post & handling	£3.80	
Total Order Cost	£	

Title of this book . . . .

I enclose a cheque/postal order for £ . . . .
made payable to 'Heritage Resource Management Ltd'

OR please debit my Mastercard / Visa / Maestro card, details below

Card Number:

Issue No (Maestro only):   Valid from (Maestro):

Card Security Number: Expires:

Signature:

Name Mr/Mrs/Ms . . . .

Address . . . .

. . . .

. . . .

. . . . Postcode . . . .

Daytime Tel No . . . .

Email . . . .

Valid to 31/12/26

Can you help us with information about any of the Frith photographs in this book?

We are gradually compiling an historical record for each of the photographs in the Frith archive. It is always fascinating to find out the names of the people shown in the pictures, as well as insights into the shops, buildings and other features depicted.

If you recognize anyone in the photographs in this book, or if you have information not already included in the author's caption, do let us know. We would love to hear from you, and will try to publish it in future books or articles.

An Invitation from The Francis Frith Collection to Share Your Memories

The 'Share Your Memories' feature of our website allows members of the public to add personal memories relating to the places featured in our photographs, or comment on others already added. Seeing a place from your past can rekindle forgotten or long held memories. Why not visit the website, find photographs of places you know well and add YOUR story for others to read and enjoy? We would love to hear from you!

www.francisfrith.com/memories

Our production team

Frith books are produced by a small dedicated team at offices near Salisbury. Most have worked with the Frith Collection for many years. All have in common one quality: they have a passion for the Frith Collection.

Frith Books and Gifts

We have a wide range of books and gifts available on our website utilising our photographic archive, many of which can be individually personalised.

www.francisfrith.com

Free Print – see overleaf

FF028711